BULANDSHAHR:

OR

SKETCHES OF AN INDIAN DISTRICT;

SOCIAL, HISTORICAL AND ARCHITECTURAL

BULANDSHAHR:

OR

SKETCHES OF AN INDIAN DISTRICT;

SOCIAL, HISTORICAL AND ARCHITECTURAL

F. S. GROWSE

GYAN

Published by

Gyan Publishing House
5, Ansari Road
Daryaganj, New Delhi-110002
Phone: 011-47034999, 9811692060
E-mail: books@gyanbooks.com

Distribution Network
gyanbooks.com
India, USA, Canada, UK, Australia

ISBN: 978-93-6780-658-6 (PB)

First Published, 1884

2nd Impression 2024

Printed at: Gyan Press, Delhi.

BULANDSHAHR
Author: F. S. GROWSE

BULANDSHAHR:

OR

SKETCHES OF AN INDIAN DISTRICT;

SOCIAL, HISTORICAL AND ARCHITECTURAL.

BY

F. S. GROWSE, C. I. E.

INDIAN CIVIL SERVICE.

WITH ILLUSTRATIONS.

"OUR WESTERN CIVILIZATION IS PERHAPS NOT ABSOLUTELY THE GLORIOUS THING WE LIKE TO IMAGINE IT." *Seeley.*

BENARES:

MEDICAL HALL PRESS.

1884.

CONTENTS.

ILLUSTRATIONS.

PREFACE.

With the exception of a few paragraphs, the whole of this little volume of district sketches has already appeared in print, Chapters I and III in the Calcutta Review and Chapter II in the Journal of the Asiatic Society of Bengal. It was intended all along that the three articles should ultimately be combined so as to form a single series, whenever the Plates that now illustrate them were ready for publication; but, as each section was separately written and made to some extent complete in itself, the result is that they seem to hang together a little loosely. The want of cohesion, however, is only in the joints of the structure and does not arise from any inherent incongruity of material. The two introductory chapters, being devoted to a general description of the district and to a history of its chief town, are a natural prelude to the third, in which all the special interest of the book is concentrated. This gives a circumstantial account of the extensive local improvements that have been carried out during the last six years, explains and defends the principles upon which the work has been conducted and urges an appeal for their wider recognition.

It was quite unnecessary for me to compile a complete and consecutive history of the district, for that has been already supplied in a highly satisfactory manner by the "Historical and statistical Memoir of Bulandshahr," written by Rájá Lachhman Siṅh and published at the Allahabad Government Press in 1874. The fragmentary character of the present monograph may be more readily condoned, if it is considered as a sequel, in which the record of administration has been continued through another decade, and only such facts have been restated as it was desired to group in a special light.

In the opinion of many competent observers, the military revolt of 1857 was largely brought about by the injudicious diminution of the personal influence and authority of commanding officers and by the transfer of their power and patronage to impersonal boards and departments. If the present system of centralization in civil affairs continues to develope, any future movement of the people at large against their rulers will be similarly assisted to a most alarming extent by the growing want of touch between the district officer and the district for which he is responsible. To use the words of Sir Frederick Weld, one of the most able and successful of our Colonial Governors: "Personal government, so far as I am competent to offer an opinion, is a necessity for Asiatics; it is the outcome of their religious systems, of their habits of thought, and of long centuries of custom." But the typical Collector is now expected to forego all personal predilections and local attachments, and to live in the roughest camp-fashion, so that he may be moved at a moment's notice from one environment to another, without occasioning any perceptible break in the continuity of office routine. Every year he becomes less and less of an independent agent and more of a registered machine, which is warranted to work with equal regularity wherever it is placed,* in absolute dependence on the winding of the departmental key. It seems to be forgotten that people are always most keenly interested in comparatively petty local affairs; if these are sympathetically administered by the local authorities, the Government can treat larger questions as it likes in the dry light of the most advanced political science, with very little risk of ever exciting popular opposition.

---

* My own career, now almost at an end, has been the exact reverse of the above picture. I have only known three districts; Mainpuri as an Assistant, Mathurá as Joint Magistrate, and Bulandshahr as Collector. Each for the time being was my home, in which all my interests were centred, and in each I have left a permanent record of my connection with the place. In Mainpuri my special contribution to local progress was the development of the art of *tárkashi*, or brass-inlaying, which I first introduced to public notice at the Agra Exhibition of 1867. Then it was treated with the greatest contempt; but in the Calcutta Exhibition of 1884 when æsthetic ideas had become more popular, my workmen were awarded a first class certificate and gold medal.

This system of minimizing the personal influence of the district officer not only contains the seeds of possible political danger in the future, but it is also fatal to the growth of social enterprize in the actual present. No oriental will exert himself except under the immediate influence of an individual leader. He likes to have his work seen and appreciated at once and has not sufficient perseverance or confidence in himself to bear up against the disappointment of a long-deferred reward. A Magistrate and Collector, who is not afraid of provoking official jealousy, and who refuses to entertain the prevalent delusion that Indian ideas, whenever they differ from European, are necessarily barbarous, will find in any district, whatever the particular bent of his own tastes may be, an ample field for beneficent action ; and he may depend upon the most generous support, provided only that it is not demanded as by a master but solicited as from a fellow-worker, and that the object is such as is calculated to conciliate native sentiment.

Neither Hindus nor Muhammadans often hoard their superfluous wealth. Either it is lavished in utter frivolities, such as fire-works and dancing girls, or it is given to so-called religious institutions, which—if Muhammadan schools—are for the most part foci of sedition, or—if Hindu temples—are hot-beds of profligacy and licentiousness. Or it may be, it is employed with less injury to morals, but with greater prejudice to æsthetic taste by the erection of such costly and hideous buildings as the Dánpur Gate, which forms the subject of one of my illustrations. If the rich native gentry can be put in a better way of spending their money, the influence exerted for this result seems to me to be well exerted.

It is objected that whatever is done under such influence is done for the sake of Government reward in the shape of a title or similar social distinction. But I believe that this is seldom the first motive. A reasonable pride in beautifying one's own town is a feeling which exists almost every where ; though it is totally ignored by the official Philistine, who has himself the true bourgeois fear of spending a Rupee on anything that is not undeniably useful. In any case, it must be more to the public advantage that a wealthy citizen should be open handed, even from an imperfect motive, than that he should stifle a generous impulse and keep his money to himself from an over righteous repugnance to ostentation. The desire of being honoured for honourable deeds is not one of the most despicable springs of human action. To perform meritorious public services and to disclaim all reward for them would be a note of higher perfection; but such altruism is superhuman; with the purest and most virtuous of men motives are always more or less mixed.

Again, it is said that the native gentry are mostly in debt and that it is wrong to encourage them to further extravagance, even if it be in well doing. But such criticism does not apply to Bulandshahr, where the landed gentry are a very wealthy class, and I doubt if it has much force anywhere. It is not public benevolence, but long-protracted litigation in the civil Courts which involves them in financial difficulties. Thus, for example, the owner of one of the largest estates in the district, Ráo Umrás Sinh of Kachesar, has given Rs. 4,500 for the erection of the handsome gate to the new public garden at Bulandshahr. This is an outlay which he will never feel and yet his name will be honourably commemorated by it on the spot, it may be for centuries. On the other hand, he has been forced into spending as much as Rs. 40,000 on barristers and pleaders, to the benefit of no other person whatever, in defending himself against a preposterous claim to a large portion of his property, which was brought against him by a low Muhammadan attorney, himself a worthy product of our highly civilized judicial system.

The suit was instituted on the 5th of August 1880, and was dismissed by the subordinate Judge as "false and fictitious and based on documents that were wholly or in part forged or fabricated." An appeal was laid in the High Court, and there, after full consideration, final judgment was pronounced containing the following and many other similar expressions of opinion: "It is impossible not to feel that the Plaintiff comes into Court under circumstances calculated to arouse suspicion, not only by reason of his extraordinary delay in preferring his claim—a delay which his counsel entirely failed to explain to our satisfaction—but because of the highly improbable and in certain respects incredible nature of many of the incidents of his story." "To express ourselves in the mildest way, we cannot but view this letter as an exceedingly suspicious document." "In short, there are in the case no original documents, because the originals were either—it is alleged—destroyed in the mutiny, or are withheld; and there is no oral proof, because all the persons, who could have deposed to any of the facts, are dead." "To ask us to believe this astounding piece of folly is no small demand upon our credulity." "The appearance of the document itself is most suspicious." "There is the gravest reason to doubt the authenticity of the signatures." "It was obvious that both these persons were telling a carefully prepared story." "We must dismiss it as wholly undeserving credence." "It is absolutely impossible to credit the plaintiff's assertion on this head." "This is a severe tax on our credulity.' "The plaintiff's statements on all these matters and his explanation of his delay in coming into Court are incredible in the highest degree." This judgment was not pronounced till July, 1883, though—as clearly appears from the above extracts—the plaintiff's case was so utterly bad that the finding of the Lower Court might have been confirmed at once, without subjecting the unfortunate victim of the conspiracy to a long-protracted three years' agony.

It is a most lamentable illustration of the total unfitness of any Indian district for independent self-government, that even in such a scandalous case as this, the plaintiff, who was an absolute pauper, was amply provided with funds by wealthy Muhammadans, simply because he was himself a Muhammadan and his attack was directed against a Hindu.

The indiscriminate abuse of English rule, in which Bengali patriots are too apt to indulge, makes it difficult to read their effusions with any degree of patience; yet it cannot be denied that there is a solid foundation in fact for the substance of their complaints, both as regards unnecessary cost in administration, and also as to the sacrifice of local to imperial interests, whenever the two come into collision. If India were governed by any other European power, there would be no pretence of disguising the fact that the dependency was held for the advantage of its rulers, and the subordinate position would probably be accepted without a murmur. It is the affectation of superior morality, which makes its occasional relapses into selfishness such an argument throughout the civilized world of the traditional perfidy of British statesmanship. It is much to be regretted that a Government which is mainly beneficent in its purpose, should wantonly damage its reputation by the obstinate maintenance of a few comparatively petty abuses, which are obvious to every one, and which from an Indian point of view it is absolutely impossible to defend. For example, an interesting indigenous art like that of the silversmith is utterly paralyzed by the retention of the customs duty and the barbarous system of hall-marking. The removal of these restrictions upon freedom of exportation would be an immense benefit to India, and in England would lead to no inconvenience beyond a slight and temporary disarrangement of a few items in the financial statement, coupled with an artistic gain to the country in the almost immediate future. Still the concession, though its justice is admitted, is indefinitely postponed. It is only India that clamours for the reform; and as India has no vote and therefore no weight in party politics, its wishes may be disregarded with impunity.

Again, there is absolutely no raison d'être for the Governors of Bombay and Madras, except that they supply the ministry with two pieces of valuable preferment; yet no Cabinet, whether Radical or Conservative, will consent to forego the patronage and so relieve India of an utterly unprofitable burden. No one will have the hardihood to assert that Bombay and Madras, though costing so much more, are either better administered than Bengal and the North-west Provinces, or are heavier and more responsible charges. A still more amazing scandal is the refusal of the Secretary of State to sanction the recommendations of the Army Commission of 1879, which would ensure increased efficiency together with an annual saving of not less than a million sterling.

Similarly, in matters of internal economy, where the Government of India, if it wished to reform, would be less hampered by parliamentary and ministerial obstructiveness. Among the greater evils of our exotic civilization are the unlimited license of appeal and the ruinous delays of the Civil Courts. But the writers for the native press mainly belong to the class that most benefits by these abuses, and therefore they are not often brought forward very prominently. More frequent topics of complaint are the constant growth of departmentalism and the multiplication of highly paid appointments for the benefit of individual Europeans, combined with a retention of all the old posts with the old salaries but with reduced responsibilities. Thus it comes about that the Magistrate and Collector of a district, ordinarily a man not less than 40 years of age and who has seen some 18 years of service, still draws the salary of a local administrator, but is treated like a head-clerk, all his responsible functions being transferred either to the Commissioner, a still more senior and more highly paid official, or to some Secretary or Department at head quarters. Most certainly I do not advocate the further effacement of the district officer, but I think that many of his new masters might be abolished and a very large saving thereby effected. Frequent ground for complaint is also found in the annual migration to the Hills, by which high officials shirk the condition of the service which they have accepted. The bracing climate of the Himalayas is no doubt more favourable than the sultry discomfort of the plains to the concoction of fussy departmental Circulars and sublimely censorious Annual Reports. But there is far too much of such literature, and it would be an incalculable blessing to the country if a little of the langour of the East—which can only be duly appreciated after a summer's sojourn in the Doáb—were occasionally allowed to temper the present *fureur de gouverner*.

Another intolerable drain on the finances of the country, combined with a great discouragement of native progress, it is the special object of this little work to expose, by showing the folly of maintaining an immense staff of highly paid European engineers for the execution of district works, which might be carried out in far better style and at much less cost by the exclusive employment of native agency.

The illustrations in the present volume are merely a sample of a much larger number that are under preparation. These I propose to publish either in a separate folio, or with a reissue of the text, at the end of the year 1885, when I shall be on the point of leaving the country. By that time I hope that all the works now in progress will have been satisfactorily completed.

F. S. GROWSE.

BULANDSHAHR,

July 12, 1884.

W. GRIGGS, PHOTO-LITH.

BULANDSHAHR MARKET-PLACE.

BULANDSHAHR.

CHAPTER I.

THE DISTRICT: ITS CHARACTERISTICS AND ITS CAPABILITIES.

THE area comprised in the present District of Bulandshahr was first administered from Aligarh, and then for a brief period from Merath, during the first twenty years after the British conquest* As a separate political unit, it dates only from the year 1824. Since then it is reckoned as one of the six Collectorates that, together, make up the Merath Division † of the North-West Provinces. It consists of an oblong tract of almost absolutely level country, which covers an extent of 1,915 square miles, being some 35 miles in breadth from north to south, with an average length of 55 miles from the banks of the Jamuná on the west, to the Ganges on the east. A third river, the *Kálindi*, more commonly called the *Káli Nadi*, ‡ runs through its centre with a south-easterly

---

* After the fall of Aligarh in 1803, the Parganas (or *Hundreds*) of Baran (*i. e.* Bulandshahr) and Khurja were first placed under Colonel Ochterlony, the Delhi Resident. In the following year they were made part of the Aligarh District, and so remained till 1818, when Baran and the other Western Parganas were transferred to Merath; but this arrangement lasted only for six years.

† Commonly spelt 'Meerut,' for which Dr. Hunter in his Imperial Gazetteer proposes to substitute 'Mirath.' This, however, would be a very unsatisfactory correction. The word is identical with 'Mertha,' the name of an ancient hill-fort in Jodhpur. The first syllable 'mer' appears as a termination in Ajmer, Jaysalmer, &c., and means 'a hill.' The old town of Merath stands on a considerable elevation, though apparently an artificial one.

‡ When the Hindi word had to be written in Persian or Urdu, the vowel in the second syllable was purposely lengthened by the Munshis in order the better to preserve its sound, and to prevent its degenerating into short *a*, as it soon would, were no vowel expressed. For a similar reason, the common Hindi termination *pur*, meaning 'town,' is always written by Munshis with a long *u*, and the short vowels *e* and *i* in English Proper names are almost invariably lengthened in the process of transliteration. The stream thus became the *Kálindi*, from which the transition was easy to the more readily intelligible *Káli nadi*, 'Black river'; the pronunciation only being altered; since the written form of the two words *Kálindi* and *Káli nadi* in Persian characters is absolutely identical. The error is of respectable antiquity, as Yahya bin Ahmad, the author of the Chronicle entitled the Táríkh-i-Mubárak Sháhi,

direction, and divides it into two almost equal portions. The Karwan, the Patwaiya and the Chúiya, are three minor water-courses, which frequently become broad and rapid torrents in the rains; at all other times of the year their bed is a mere shallow depression in the soil, with scarcely distinguishable banks, and is generally brought under cultivation. At some remote period, there seems reason to believe, the Chúiya was a permanent stream, of much greater importance than now; for the sites of several ancient towns and forts, as at Chandokh, Indor, Chimávali and Dibhái, can be traced on its banks; and recently, on sinking a well in its bed, the soil at a depth of 33 feet was found to be full of small shells. It probably depended for existence on the primæval forests, and gradually dwindled away as they were cut down. It still occasionally asserts its old strength, and on the 19th of September 1880, it suddenly rose and swept away a large masonry bridge, near the town of Dibhái, which the Public Works Department had finished only a few months previously.

Since the suppression of the Mutiny in 1858, Buland shahr, for administrative purposes, has been entirely separated from Delhi, which now forms part of another Province, the Panjáb. But the historical and social connection between the two localities is not so easily to be severed. The towers and domes of the ancient metropolis are visible from the border of the district, and in modern, no less than in pre-historic, times the special characteristics of the neighbourhood are mainly due to the action of Imperial influences.

According to tradition, the original seat of the earliest Hindu dynasty—which proudly traced its descent from the mythical Regent of the Moon—was at Hastinapur, a name that still survives, but attaches only to a desolate group of shapeless mounds overlooking the old bed of the Ganges, some twenty-two miles north-east of the Merath Cantonments. When king Dhritaráshtra divided his dominions between his hundred sons and five nephews, the latter, still famous in popular speech under their names of the Pándavas, founded Indra-prastha (now Indra-pat, or old Delhi) as one of their capitals, and gradually cleared the surrounding country both

---

written about the year 1450, translates the name into Persian by the phrase *Áb-i-Siyáh, i. e.* Black-water. It rises in Muzaffarnagar, flows through Merath into Bulandshahr, and thence after traversing Aligarh, Eta and Farrukhabad, falls into the Ganges about half way between the towns of Farrukhabad and Cawnpur.

of its primæval forest and of the wild Nága tribes, who had made it their stronghold. On the termination of the internecine struggle, which forms the subject of the Mahábhárat, Yudhishthir, the last of the five brothers, again united the divided realm. He in course of time was succeeded on the throne of Hastinapur by Paríkshit, the grandson of his brother Arjun; and to Paríkshit's son, Janmejaya, is ascribed the foundation of Ahár, the oldest town in the district, from which he sent out a colony to build the fort of Baran, the modern Bulandshahr.

Thus, to Delhi chieftains are due the first reclamation of the soil and the first establishment of a social community, more than three thousand years ago: while at the present day the local magnates, more numerous here than in any other part of the province, are for the most part the descendants of Delhi courtiers, who obtained grants of land from the Emperors, either in recognition of their submission to the faith, or in reward for military services.

Thus the ancestor of the Biluch family at Jhájhar, now almost ruined by waste and litigation, was a companion-in-arms of Humáyun; another Biluch family, seated at Chanderu, rose into importance as local governors under Aurangzeb, and a century later acquired the village where they now reside, as a reward for services against the Mahrattas; the wealthy and influential Lál Kháni family, now headed by the two Nawàbs of Chhatári and Pahásu, and owning more than 200 villages in this and the adjoining districts, are descended from a Thakur of the Bargùjar clan, who abjured Hinduism under Aurangzeb's imperial persuasion; the Patháns of Jahángirabad were connected with one of the principal commanders of the Mughal troops in the reign of Sháh Alam, and subsequently obtained a grant of land from Lord Lake; and, lastly—though the list might be considerably extended—to come down to the present day, the nucleus of the handsome estate now enjoyed by the fine old Afghan soldier, Saiyid Mír Khán, better known as the Sardár Bahádur, was won by his gallantry in the Kábul war, and was augmented in acknowledgment of his distinguished loyalty in the Mutiny.

The proximity to the Muhammadan centre of Government has not only largely affected the character of the entire population in the lower as well as in the higher classes, but has also had a considerable influence on the general aspect of the landscape. In dress, language, and caste-prejudices there is a conspicuous relaxation of customary Hindu usage, and till within the last few years, though every considerable village boasted a mosque of more or less pretension, a Hindu spire was seldom visible; the cry of the Muazzin had all but completely silenced the clang of the temple-bell and the boom of the devotee's conch. Now, that no active demonstration of religious intolerance is permitted, and every sect is allowed to practise its own rites and ceremonies, under the equal protection of the law, it is not to be expected but that the Hindus, who number 748,256 out of a total population of 924,822, will gradually begin to re-assert themselves. The trade of the towns is entirely in their hands, but the prestige that attaches to ownership of the land is mainly on the side of Islám. Though the surface of the stream may appear abnormally smooth, there is a strong under-current of jealousy, faction and intrigue, which rash experiments in administration would speedily develop into a very real danger.

In point of population, as recorded by the census of 1881, the district stands sixteenth in the list of 49 which, together, constitute the United Provinces. But by the License Tax assessments, which are the most trustworthy test of general prosperity, it comes as high as fourth, having only Cawnpur, Merath and Aligarh above it. This remarkable pre-eminence is due to a variety of causes, the principal being the lightness of the Government demand under the head of land revenue. The existing settlement was introduced in 1865, and will expire in 1889; when it is estimated that the demand will advance from a little over 13½ lakhs to at least 18. This event is naturally anticipated by the landlords with some little perturbation; but while they appreciate the manifold advantages to themselves of the present golden age, they also recognise the right of the State to participate in the general increase of agricultural well-being. Great attention has been paid by the staff of district officials to the maintenance of the village maps and records of crops and rents, and—when the time comes for the new assessment—it is hoped that these papers will form a sufficient basis for all the necessary calculations. If so, the Government will save the large cost of a special establishment for a period of several years (the present settlement and its revision lasted from 1856 to 1870!) the people will escape a vast amount of annoyance and litigation, and the land will not be thrown out of cultivation, or denied improvements, in the fraudulent hope of concealing its capabilities. In no district as yet has any such summary procedure been found possible; if it is sanctioned for Bulandshahr, and works well, it will be a matter for unqualified congratulation.

Cereals are the great staple of the country; but there are also nearly 68,000 acres under cotton, while the number of indigo factories has now risen to 195. The soil, which is naturally fertile, and of very uniform character, has the further advantage of almost universal protection from drought; being largely capable of artificial irrigation from the distributories of the Ganges Canal. This flows through the whole breadth of the district in three wide and nearly parallel branches, one to the east, the other two to the west of the central Kálindi. Thus, the terrible famine of 1877 was here almost unfelt. No poor-houses or relief works had to be started by Government, nor had any steps to be taken to stimulate the importation of food-stuffs. The grain accumulated in more prosperous seasons, was extracted from the pits in which it had been buried, and sold greatly to the profit of the dealer, but at the same time, not at utterly prohibitory prices; while the credit of the tenant still remained so good, that he was able, if necessary, to negotiate a temporary loan without permanent embarrassment. Gangs of starving vagrants from Mathura, Bharatpur, and other centres of distress, plodded along the main roads; but the able bodied among them gradually found work in the Municipalities or elsewhere, and the utterly helpless were kept alive by the daily dole of food that was freely given by the larger landed proprietors in the villages, and by wealthy traders in the towns. It may, therefore, be considered as established by a recent and crucial test, that the district is practically secure against any ordinary calamity. But to map out the entire area—as has been proposed—in deeper and lighter shades of color according to a nice calculation of possibilities, and to determine, once for all, that such and such tracts will be entitled to relief in time of drought, and that others can always do without it, seems as unpractical a project as an attempt to construct a permanent chart of the clouds in the sky. If accurate observations are maintained, the occurrence of a storm and its probable intensity may be predicted, and precautions taken to minimize the danger; but circumstances must be treated as they arise, and no region in the world, by virtue of long previous exemption from misfortunes, can be marked off as absolutely secure for ever from special visitations of

Providence. Inflexible routine may be a welcome support to a feeble administrator, but it is simply an embarrassment to a competent one; while legislation in itself is always an evil, and our Indian land-laws, above all, have had the disastrous effect of inflicting permanent injury on the class whom they were chiefly intended to benefit. When left to their own good feelings, the landlords, as a rule, are disposed to treat their tenants, in time of difficulty, with the same liberality that they exhibit in the other ordinary relations of life; it is only when the law confronts them with its rigid impersonality that they refuse to listen any longer to the voice of equity.

The great curse of the district is the prevalence of fever, an evil which must in part be attributed to what is otherwise so signal a boon,*—the large extension of canal irrigation. In the autumn of 1879, an unusually heavy rainfall, following upon several years of drought, developed a terrible epidemic, which literally more than decimated the population. The crops stood uncut in the fields, the shops remained closed in the bazars; there was no traffic along the high roads, and no hum of business in the market-places; the receding flood of the great rivers showed their sands piled with corpses, while scarcely a water-course or wayside ditch but contained some ghastly relics of humanity, hastily dropt by hireling bearers or even by friends, too fearful for themselves, or too enfeebled by sickness to observe the funeral rites that are ordinarily held so sacred. In most of the towns and villages there was not a single house in which there was not one dead; in many, entire families had perished—parents, grand-parents and children—and whole streets became deserted. Probably, not a thousand people in all, from one end of the district to the other, escaped without some touch of the disease. The Pargana least affected was Ahár, which then by equitable decree enjoyed its compensation for many permanent disadvantages. It is a narrow tract of country, running along the high bank of the Ganges, with a poor soil inadequately watered and ill

* The North-Western Provinces have now 30,000 square miles, in which the arrival of a famine will, instead of bringing desolation and ruin, merely ensure an especially prosperous season for the fortunate proprietors of irrigated land. When the provincial system of railways is complete, and the Bhopal-Jhansi line to Cawnpur and Agra has triumphed over the obstinate procrastination of the India Office, 1,500 square miles under canal-irrigated wheat and barley ought to go far towards rendering this part of the country secure, whatever be the delay in the south-west monsoon, or the caprices of the winter rains.

provided with roads, and which thus offers no attractions for the investment of capital on the part either of traders or land-owners.

As a result of the general mortality, the population which had been 937,427 in 1871, and since then had largely increased, fell in 1881 to 924,882; the solitary town in the whole district which showed any augmentation being Bulandshahr itself, which rose from 14,804 to 17,863. Still, distressing as it was at the time, the epidemic ran its course and left no lasting ill effects behind. On the contrary, the result was rather one of relief from overcrowding, and when the period of depression had passed, a large increase in the birth-rate showed that it was chiefly the very old, or young or infirm, who had been removed, and that the actual vigour of the community remained unimpaired.

Much has been done of late years by the irrigation department to correct the excessive humidity which has been caused by their canals, and extensive schemes for the relief of the most low-lying and water-logged lands have either been carried out or are still in progress. As many as 186 miles of drainage cuts have been excavated; the Kálindi has been straightened and kept within its banks, at a cost of Rs. 94,757; and similar operations estimated to cost Rs. 37,800, are now being commenced on the Karwan. The only portion of the district where artificial drainage is still required is the Jewar Pargana, and for this a provision of Rs. 20,000 has been made. To complete the project, however, it will be necessary to improve the bed of the Patwaiya, which will involve a further outlay.

All this must have a beneficial effect on the general atmosphere; but the special conditions of the towns and villages are so unfavourable, that many years must elapse before any marked improvement can be expected in their vital statistics. The whole surface of the country is a dead level, with the population massed in artificial depressions, which have been dug to supply the earth for building purposes. The houses, instead of being raised—as sanitary laws would require—are sunk some two or three feet below the level of the ground, and the sides of the pit form the basement of the walls. To complete the necessary height, mud is mixed and brought in from any waste spot near at hand. The result is, that the village itself stands in a hole, and is hemmed in by an irregular circle of trenches used as receptacles for every kind of abomination. Add to this, that herds of cattle every evening return to the homestead, and during the night share the same quarters with their masters. The soil is thus in the course of years saturated with impurities, and, as it is the custom to sleep either on the ground or on a very low pallet, it is no matter for surprise that the annual victims of fever are more than of all other diseases combined.

In the majority of cases it is not altogether poverty that is responsible for the utter want of domestic comfort, but rather an apathetic acquiescence in a degraded standard of social life arising from ignorance that anything better is obtainable. The characteristic oriental craving for decoration is frequently indicated by the carving of the wooden eaves and brackets and by the plaster niches and mouldings of the doorways, which, though rude in execution, are often of appropriate and picturesque design ; but there is no appreciation whatever of cleanliness or ventilation, and no effort is made to secure them. In a really rich man's house the latter defect is equally conspicuous ; the courtyards are larger and the buildings are more substantial, but the arrangements for conservancy are not a whit better, and there is generally much less evidence of taste, in consequence of a vicious tendency to abandon the indigenous style and copy the hideous vulgarisms of the Public Works Department. Before the people of India can claim to rank on an equality with Europeans, it is above all things necessary that they should reform their domestic habits of life: when they have learnt to order these matters aright, their political enfranchisement will follow spontaneously on their capacity for it; the reverse process must be unreal and can only eventuate in failure.

Next to the unhealthy condition of their homes, the two institutions that most conduce to the propagation of disease are pilgrimages and marriage-feasts. Both practices have their root in the intolerable monotony of ordinary existence, which grasps at any change for a relief, but disguises the real motive by an affectation of religious or social obligation. Closely packed in bullock carts or some other equally clumsy vehicle, the guests start in straggling procession, and jog along the weary roads for the distance of a hundred miles or more, halting only for an hour or two at an occasional well for a draught of water and a mouthful of parched grain. Aching in every limb from the jolting of the springless cart and the cramped position into which they have been squeezed, choked with dust, dizzy from the glare of the sun and want of sufficient food—for they purposely starve themselves in order to do more justice to the feast—they at last arrive at their journey's end. Here no accommodation has been provided for them, and no amusement, beyond enormous piles of indigestible food, with which they gorge themselves without intermission for three days and nights, freely abusing their host, should there be any shortcoming, and then start on the homeward journey, to endure the same discomforts as before, now aggravated by the agonies of indigestion. Every year half the outbreaks of cholera that occur may be traced up to these ghastly merry-makings. At pilgrimages there is no over-eating, but the exposure and the crowding are greater, and an essential part of the proceedings generally consists in drinking some filthy water from a turbid stream or stagnant tank of reputed sanctity, where thousands of people have been bathing. On neither occasion is there any thought of pleasing the eye or gratifying the mind, except by the excitement inseparable from being one of a crowd which is moved by a common object.

If the sordid discomfort of home were relieved by some element of culture, people would no longer look abroad for their enjoyments. They would be happier and healthier, nor would the ultimate cost of living be increased. Instead of money being hoarded for special occasions, and then squandered in thankless and unprofitable profusion, it would be distributed with judicious economy over the whole area of domestic requirements. Food, clothing, shelter and education are comparatively so cheap, that all but the very poorest could rear a family in a decent and respectable manner, if it were not for the extravagant outlay on marriages. The various attempts that have been made to enforce the reduction of such expenses are well-meaning, but have not achieved much success, nor do I think they are ever likely to do so. The root of the evil lies deeper, and it is that which has to be attacked. Make the general aspect of life more attractive, and there will then be less desire to smirch it with crude blotches of colour.

The recent advance in the general prosperity of the district has been faithfully reflected step by step and year after year in the annual Criminal Returns; for in India, as in England, to use the words of Tennyson's Northern Farmer, 'Tisn't them as has money that breaks into houses and steals." But anomalies of all kinds, however gratifying may be the exceptional circumstances which they indicate, are always *per se* displeasing to the compiler of statistics at head-quarters; for he has no personal concern with the facts, and is interested only in the symmetrical appearance of the figures exhibited in his tabular statements. A conventional explanation of the discrepancy has therefore to be found in an alleged concealment of offences. There is, however, no good reason for supposing that the people are more unwilling here than elsewhere to invoke the assistance of the Police for the recovery of stolen property, or the redress of any real injury. A murder or a burglary can scarcely be committed without attracting attention, and if in the case of petty disputes there is a reluctance to waste time and money by coming into court about them, such a habit of mind is rather to be encouraged than condemned.*

Another matter in which the district falls short of official requirements is the consumption of spirituous liquor. Temperance is a virtue, in which the excise authorities are by no means ready to believe. If the revenue is not up to the ordinary standard, the only explanation of the fact that they will accept is smuggling. But in spite of exceptional vigilance, an evasion of the law is very rarely detected, and probably is rarely practised. The absence of drunkenness and the absence of crime go together and explain each other. If a tempting array of bottles were displayed at selected spots along the most frequented thoroughfares, many a dusty pedestrian might be induced to assuage his thirst with a draught, and so acquire a taste which would eventually be beneficial to the excise revenue. A similar result might follow from an increase of the number of drinking-shops in the towns and large villages, to serve as social clubs for the dissolute; but the advantage to the respectable community may be doubted, while the gain to Government would be more than counterbalanced by the charges of extra police and increased jail accommodation.

---

* It is satisfactory to observe that the altered condition of things has at last been recognized. Mr. Webster, the Inspector-General of Police, who was Magistrate of Bulandshahr from 1863 to 1866, writes as follows in his review of the year 1882:—"The circumstances of the people have changed greatly. They are far more prosperous than they were; cultivation has greatly extended, and large tracts which were grass jungles when I knew the district, and which harboured cattle-stealers and their booty, are now well-cultivated corn-lands; and what is more important as regards the cessation of crime, the very persons who used these lands as asylums in their thieving forages are now the cultivators of them. The Gújars, who used to commit at least a third of all the crime in the district, are now to a certain extent reformed, and only occasionally vary their agricultural pursuits by an expedition for the purposes of cattle or other theft."

With a large number of wealthy landed proprietors, mostly Muhammadans, living on their own estate, in the midst of their own tenantry, as many as thirteen of them exercising the powers of Honorary Magistrates and ready to report any suspicious circumstance they may observe; with the whole population singularly well-to-do and largely impregnated with Muhammadan ideas of social propriety; and with whole tribes ordinarily reputed criminal, forsaking their old predatory habits for the more assured profits of honest husbandry, it would be strange indeed, if the district statistics coincided precisely with those of other localities where industry and sobriety are not so conspicuously remunerative.

In addition to the many advantages already enumerated, the district is well provided with communications, having as many as seven Railway Stations, four on the East Indian and three on the Oudh and Rohilkhand line. It is also traversed by the Grand Trunk Road from the Aligarh to the Delhi border, and has a complete net-work of minor thoroughfares radiating in every direction from the town of Bulandshahr, which occupies the exact centre of the whole area. A few years ago, during one of the periodical financial panics, several of the roads were summarily condemned by the head of the Public Works Department, and broken up at considerable expense; but their reconstruction will be one of the first acts of the new Local Committee. The greatest obstacle to freedom of communication has hitherto been the Kálindi, which had a permanent bridge only at Bulandshahr, and no bridge or ferry of any kind whatever between that town and Hápur in the Merath district, a distance of about 30 miles. As the banks are high and sudden floods frequent, it was never safe for a traveller to reckon on the possibility of a passage, and the obstruction to traffic was thus most serious. This has now been removed by the munificence of one of the Honorary Magistrates, Saiyid Mihrbán Ali, who has constructed a substantial bridge of twenty-three arches, near the town of Guláothi, where his residence is, at the large cost of Rs. 30,000.

My letter to the Secretary to Government, in which I first broached the scheme of this Bridge, was dated 7 January 1881. I quote it at length, since the correspondence illustrates in a forcible manner the almost inconceivable insolence and obstructiveness of the Department to which the material progress of the country is mainly entrusted.

It ran as follows:

"This district, as you are aware, is divided into two nearly equal portions by the Kálindi river, which runs from north to south right through the middle of it. Between Hápur in the Merath district and the town of Bulandshahr, there is not a single bridge of any kind, nor even a ferry, and the consequent inconvenience (as you may imagine) is very great—the more so as an old thoroughfare runs from the town of Guláothi on the Merath and Aligarh road to Sayána near the Ganges and thence on to Garhmuktesvar—which would be very largely used, but for the uncertainty that always exists as to the possibility of getting across the river. Every cold weather that I have been in the district, I have found it impassable for carts, and when in the neighbourhood of Guláothi have been obliged to return all the way to Bulandshahr before I could reach Agota, which lies immediately opposite on the left-bank of the stream, thus making the distance 25 miles instead of something less than 5. Previous Collectors have urged the matter upon the notice of Government, but it has always been shelved, mainly I suppose on account of want of funds. I myself also wrote on the subject soon after I had taken over charge of the district, and represented that several of the land-owners in the neighbourhood had volunteered to contribute to the cost, but the correspondence came to nothing, the D. P. W. in their refusal to act insisting chiefly upon the want of statistics with regard to the number of people using the Guláothi and Sayána road; an absurdity which I can only compare to the question of how many steamers passed through the Isthmus of Suez before the canal was dug.

"However, though Government assistance has been refused, it now seems likely that this important work will be undertaken by private munificence. A few days ago, Munshi Mihrbán Ali, Rais and Honorary Magistrate of Guláothi, was calling upon me and, after mentioning that he always set apart a portion of his annual income for religious and charitable purposes, he went on to say that he had now a considerable sum in hand as to the disposal of which he had formed and rejected various schemes, but he had finally come to the conclusion that he could not spend it in any way more likely to perpetuate his name (he has no son) or benefit his neighbours than by building a bridge over the Kalindi on the Guláothi and Sayána road. The offer, I should explain, was entirely spontaneous and I had said nothing whatever to prompt it. I at once warmly approved of the idea and he then asked me to make the necessary arrangements and obtain Government sanction—his only condition being that the work should be carried out under my general supervision without any interference on the part of the D. P. W. whose bridges in this neighbourhood, notwithstanding their great cost, have been any thing but successful; three have been swept away during the last two years, one of them only a few months after it was finished.

"As the Munshi himself will be the only loser, if the bridge is a failure, while in case of success the boon to the public will be very great, I should have submitted the proposal formally through the Commissioner in the certain expectation that it would be brought favourably to the notice of Government, had I not been already warned by past experience—as I will proceed to explain. On the actual boundary line of the Bulandshahr and Aligarh districts, the Oudh and Rohilkhand Railway has a station called Atrauli Road, which is absolutely useless for want of any approach to it. The Aligarh and Anupshahr high road runs at a distance of a few miles from it, but the branch connecting it with the station is absolutely impassable even for the very roughest wheeled vehicle. The inconvenience being so great, Raja Bákir Ali Khán of Pindrawal, a village half way between the station and the high road, with an amount of public spirit that I thought did him great credit, volunteered to metal the entire length at his own expense and to keep it permanently in repair. Unless the circumstances have already come to your knowledge, I think you will scarcely believe that the offer, which I duly represented to the Commissioner, was treated with an utter want of courtesy and was finally after much delay unceremoniously refused, simply because the Raja wished to carry out the work himself and not through the agency of the Public Works.

"Warned by this experience, and not wishing to subject Mihrbán Ali to a similar rebuff, I write thus informally to you in the first instance, in the hope that you will be kind enough to mention the matter to His Honour and secure his general approval, before further steps are taken.

"The example once set, I fancy it will find at least one imitator; for about a year ago, Sir Faiz Ali Khán sounded me about building a bridge over the same river near Pahású—which would also be a great public benefit—but I had been too much annoyed by the Atrauli Road affair which was then fresh in my mind, to give him much encouragement."

A gracious reply was inmediately receiv ed to the effect that H. H. the Lieut. Governor was prepared unhesitatingly to accept and commend the public spirited offer, provided the Chief Engineer in the D. P. W. was satisfied that the Bridge was not likely to do mischief to the country up stream, by damming up flood water. If his opinion on this point was satisfactory, the Public Works would have no further concern with the undertaking and it might be executed as I and the donor thought best. The proposed design was at once forwarded to the Executive Engineer, but he, in despite of the express instructions of Government to the contrary, persisted in calling for minute information on a variety of matters entirely unconnected with the question of water way, suggesting the entertainment of a professional Surveyor, for whose pay a deposit should be made, and writing generally in such an unpleasant style that at last, on June 1, I again addressed the Government direct, representing that when a spontaneous offer had been made of a munificent gift, it was at least uncourteous, if not absolutely insulting to throw doubt on the good faith of the donor and to demand a guarantee of the immediate fulfilment of his promise; that collection of materials was progressing and that the work would certainly be started directly sanction was accorded. This, however, was not communicated for another 6 months, when at last on the 9 January 1882, Col. Peile, the Chief Engineer, grudgingly admitted that "he thought the 207 superficial feet proposed would suffice to pass the river without inconveniently obstructing it;" but even so he could not refrain from concluding with a paragraph of gross impertinence to myself. Now that the work is completed, the officers of the Department criticise the design for its extravagant water way. The excess however was intentional. If the slightest question could have been raised as to sufficiency on this point, the commencement of the work would have been indefinitely postponed and finally dropped altogether, after I had left the district. All that the Chief Engineer could bring himself to say regarding the proposed water way, though he must have been aware that it was larger than circumstances required, was that he did not *think* there would be any *inconvenient* obstruction.

In such a quiet and prosperous part of the country, where there is no great injustice to correct, or practical grievance to remedy, it seems the height of unwisdom to be for ever introducing new laws and systems of administration, which, however admirable in theory, have never been recognized as wants by the people themselves. What they require of Government is the strong maintenance of order, and the persistent extension of material improvements. These are boons which they can understand and appreciate far more highly than the invidiousness of the franchise and the anarchy of self-Government. Under sympathetic guidance, they are capable of great and rapid advance, but without direction of some sort, they are absolutely powerless. They can admire action in others, but without a strong stimulus are loth to engage in it themselves; their philosophic literature shows that they can rival the profoundest German professor in tracking the abysses of transcendental speculation; and with a little practice there can be no doubt that they would soon become as expert as a Frenchman in the elaboration of paper constitutions, and the technical conduct of a debating society; but in the palmiest days of their independence they never had a metalled road in the largest of their cities, nor a swinging punkha in the most luxurious of their palaces. And these are the typical blessings, which it is the province of the British Government to supply.

In the matter of school education, official efforts have not been attended with very brilliant success. The real civilizing influences, that within the last few years have so largely modified the thoughts and habits of the people, have been the Post and the Railway. Their beneficial stimulus has been felt universally; while the effect of our schools has been limited to a single class, and that numerically the smallest and politically the least important. Every head of a department is beset by a crowd of applicants for clerical employ, who have been taught at the public expense to read and write in the Persian character, and who consider that they have thus established a claim to maintenance for life in some Government office. Certainly, their acquirements would not often stand them in much stead in any other vocation. They have never learnt to think, and have totally lost both the faculty of observation and the instinctive propriety of taste which in the uneducated Oriental so often compensate for the want of scholastic training.

Unfortunately, the curriculum of our schools is not calculated to satisfy the modest requirements of the yeoman, the artizan, the trader, and generally the independent middle classes, which ought to supply the material for those local boards which the Government is now so anxious to organize.

What primary instruction is given is not regarded as a possible end in itself, but only as a means to passing an examination. A little reflection must show that this is exactly the reverse of what is wanted. Instead of a teacher priding himself on the number of his pupils, who have got Government appointments, it would be far more to the purpose if he could boast a long list of boys who, after learning to read, write, and cypher, had settled down contentedly to their hereditary occupations, and had proved the value of education by turning out their work in a more intelligent style than their fathers had done before them. This would be a guarantee of genuine progress, and would check that rapid decay of all indigenous arts and manufactures which is the necessary result of our pernicious system of schooling, which aims at converting all the rising generation into mere office clerks.

There is no occasion whatever for the Government to take up this line of business. If all our village schools were to be closed to-morrow, the only function they adequately discharge, *viz.*, the training of Munshis for Government service, would be carried on by private enterprise with much the same results as at present. A craving for vernacular education by people who can earn their bread without it is the very last want that is felt by an ordinary community. There were schools for teaching Latin in England for centuries before the idea was entertained that the masses required to be taught English. A similar superstition survives in India, and we encourage it by our village schools for Persian and Urdu. We exhaust the resources of Government in making a free gift of professional training to people who are quite able to provide it for themselves, instead of applying all our means to the diffusion of a simple vernacular education, far more important in its effects on national progress, but less productive of immediate individual advancement, and therefore at once more deserving of, and more dependent on, State patronage. Even in such a Muhammadanized district as that in which I am writing, more than half the members of the different municipal committees can read only the true vernacular character of the country, *i e.*, the Nágari. In the proposed rural tahsili committees the proportion would be still higher. Such men, having never been brought under the influence of our schools, cannot undertake the management of affairs in accordance with European ideas, and are necessarily quite unable to follow and check intricate accounts which are kept only in Persian and English. If left to themselves, they will either do nothing, or else, in all that they do, they will be absolutely at the mercy of their paid clerk.

The remedies that I would propose for these admitted evils, are two. In the first place, I would do away with the present system of Government inspection and put the primary schools of every district under the absolute control of the local committee, at the same time increasing the staff of the Deputy Inspectors,—who would then be Deputies no longer—and the Sub-Inspectors. Not only, as has often been pointed out, are the Inspectors much too highly cultivated for the drudgery that devolves upon them, but in every country Government inspection has the inevitable result of raising the standard, which in primary schools is exactly what is not wanted. The effect of the Education Act of 1870 in England is vitiated by the same incurable tendency : the Board schools, which were intended for the poor, have gradually become suitable only for the lower middle classes, for whose benefit it was quite unnecessary that the whole community should be taxed. Secondly, the only character that I would allow to be taught in primary schools is the Nágari. This—to say the least—answers as well as any other for all the ordinary requirements of rural life, and it has the special advantage that it does not qualify for any kind of Government service. The Persian character would be taught, as now, in the pargana and tahsili schools, and boys who wished to learn it could proceed there, after undergoing the prescribed course of instruction in the primary school. It appears to me that nothing could be more equitable than this arrangement : Hindus would be gratified by having Hindi recognized as the basis of the vernacular, while the Muhammadan phase of the language would still retain the stamp of official currency.

As regards the language question, I have no patience with the continued use of the fantastic word Urdu. What people talk all over these provinces is Hindustani, which, when *written*, takes a Persianized form among Muhammadans and a Hindi form among Hindus. In both phases it has a Hindi basis, which cannot be got rid of even in the most artificial Urdu ; on the other hand, a multitude of Persian words have been naturalized in its common vocabulary, which even in Hindi it would be pedantic to ignore. As it is already the general medium of intercourse throughout India, all Indian races may eventually be brought to accept it, and therefore the recognition of a multiplicity of spoken dialects as distinct literary languages is much to be deprecated. The best means of checking the growing divergence between Hindustani and the vernaculars of other parts of

India would perhaps be found in the institution of an academy of orientalists, who would authoritatively settle the renderings to be adopted for new terms of European art and science. But the universal acceptance of a neutralized Hindustani, involving a complete reconciliation between Urdu and Hindi, can only be effected in one way. So long as the vernacular of the N.-W. P. is written by Munshis in the Persian, and by Pandits in the Nágari character, it is utterly impossible that purism should be eradicated. The one party will indent on Persian and Arabic for their vocabulary, the other on Sanskrit ; and though the grammatical structure may be much the same in both compositions, neither of the two will be intelligible to the writer of the other. The adoption of the Roman character would at once remove the whole difficulty ; and if it were introduced in our schools, it would rapidly, without any forcing, supersede both its rivals as the vehicle for ordinary written communication.

I have already alluded to the decay of native arts and manufactures, for which our faulty system of education is partly responsible. Something is being done towards their revival by Schools of Design, as at Lahor, Bombay and elsewhere, and by local Exhibitions. But, so long as the dreadful upas tree of the Public Works Department is allowed to overshadow the country, sporadic efforts like these can have no perceptible effect on popular culture. Architecture is the first of all the decorative arts, and its degradation paralyses them all. Our public buildings, which with scarcely an exception are either ludicrously mean or obtrusively hideous, now occupy conspicuous positions in every station and municipality, and, being naturally accepted as models for imitation, are rapidly accustoming the native eye to what is vulgar and tasteless. What weight in the opposite scale can be attributed to the teaching of a few schools or an occasional grant for the restoration of an ancient palace or temple ? If there is really a desire to revive oriental art, I believe it can be done without the fussy agency of a department and without any expense to the State, simply by allowing municipal committees to erect their own buildings, to make each Town Hall an emporium of local industry, and generally to develope indigenous talent by the exercise of judicious patronage. In technical as well as in the higher literary education, I believe that a healthy influence can be exerted by Government only from the outside, by removing artificial restrictions and encouraging spontaneous action. In primary education, on the other hand, the whole burden must fall on the State; but, by a simplification of the machinery, the cost and labour may be rendered much less than at present and the outturn much larger and of a more durable quality.

A notable stimulus has been given to the indigenous industries of the district by a local Show, which was started by a former Collector, Mr. Willock, in 1873. It is supported by voluntary subscriptions, which amount every year to upwards of Rs. 4,000. As a horse fair, it has succeeded so well, that it now receives an annual Government grant of Rs. 1,250 for prizes, and attracts remount officers from all parts of India.* As regards agricultural produce, greater care is taken than before in the selection of grain for seed, so that Bulandshahr wheat is very largely exported and is quoted at high prices in the London market. Attention to the subject of cattle breeding is encouraged by a special Government grant of Rs. 100, but no improvement has yet been effected. As fodder becomes every year scarcer and dearer, the people must gradually reduce the extravagant number of miserable half-starved animals that they are now in the habit of keeping. With a smaller stock, of better quality, the compulsory reservation of grazing ground in every village will be most beneficial; but if it is started immediately, before the small farmers have fully realized how impossible it is for them, under the altered circumstances of the country, to support a large herd in good condition, the effect will probably be only to intensify the present evil. Until the breed of cattle has been improved, it is premature to attempt any improvement in the native plough. The arts and manufactures represented at the district show were, till lately, ludicrous and puerile. This department has now made great bounds: the Sikandarabad muslins, the Jewar *durries* and rugs, the Khurja pottery, the Jahangirabad cotton-prints and the Bulandshahr wood-carving are revivals or developments which are achieving a more than local reputation. The specimens exhibited in the Calcutta Exhibition of 1884 were awarded three prizes, including a gold medal and first class certificate.

In every kind of district work my experience is that the normal Government grants are extremely liberal and quite ample for the purpose. But the expenditure is so hampered and embarrassed by departmental

* There are fiive stables in the district, at Malikpur, Baroli, Charávak, Bulandshahr and Masota, with stalls for seven Government stallions. Four of the horses are Norfolk Trotters, two thorough-bred English, and one an Arab. Donkeys are also kept for mule-breeding.

interference, that foresight and economy are impossible, and systematic waste of course results in chronic impecuniosity. If in a native State, administration is ruined by caprice, still more so is it in British India by routine and returns. This is most conspicuously illustrated by the department of Public Works. For large imperial undertakings, such as railways, bridges over the great rivers, military roads extending the whole length of the province, and barracks for European soldiers, it is desirable to maintain an adequate staff of European Engineers. But for the ordinary requirements of a civil district, local native talent would be not only more economical, but also more efficient. The masons who reared the tombs and palaces that are still the most notable sights in the country, have direct descendants at the present day, in the creators, for instance, of modern Mathurá, which dates entirely from the beginning of this century, and justly ranks as one of the handsomest cities in northern India. If men of this stamp were allowed to design and execute our district buildings, the promotion of indigenous industry would become—so far—a reality, instead of a transparent fiction as hitherto. The only difficulty lies in their inability to satisfy departmental requirements in the matter of tabular statements and returns. These are based on an intricate and voluminous system of checks and counterchecks, which it requires some years' training to master, and assiduous labour to maintain. The entire energy of the whole establishment is concentrated on the manipulation of the accounts and the works are left to look after themselves. However badly the latter may turn out, if only they cost enough, they will make an imposing show on paper at the year's end, and will be regarded with complete satisfaction by the supreme authorities. For example, the completion of an embankment along the right bank of the Kálindi for the protection of the town of Bulandshahr, was specially mentioned in an annual report as an important work of public utility. The cost was Rs. 4,000 : it was not added, perhaps it was not known, that the actual benefit was less than *nil*. In order to construct it, earth was dug from the town side, and the level of the ground was thus reduced below that of the bed of the river. The result was that for some years the drainage from the surrounding country collected, as in a basin, and was barred from all escape. The nuisance was partially remedied by the great flood of 1880, which breached the embankment in several places, thus proving it to be as powerless against the river in exceptional seasons, as it was effective for mischief in ordinary years.

This is a fair sample of the injurious results of a policy which entrusts district works to irresponsible provincial agency; irresponsible, because the local authorities are powerless to interfere, while the departmental authorities—sublimely indifferent to such petty undertakings—see only the neatly tabulated entries in the official return, and these they complacently pass as quite *en regle*. Besides the embankment and some new barracks in the jail, the only other original work that has been executed by professional engineers during my tenure of office in this district, is the bridge, which, as already mentioned, fell down a few months after it was finished. In the extensive series of improvements, which in the course of five years have converted a mean village into a handsome town, the department has had no hand whatever, except that it greatly delayed their commencement by representing to the Government, with stupendous effrontery, that the result would be "an eye-sore."

Facts will never run off so smoothly as mathematical abstractions, and, therefore, to avoid friction, it is generally found advisable to adhere to the latter. The district officer signs these fancy documents by scores at a time, in duplicate or triplicate, at the top or the bottom, on the face or the reverse, in the blank spaces indicated by the engineer, and can only hope they are technically correct; for the purposes of actual check he keeps a simple statement of his own, which may be very unscientific, but is as least intelligible. About the middle of the month, when the returns have all been despatched and objections answered, the European Engineer feels a little at leisure, and drives out to see the bridge, or road, that may be in progress, gives a few hurried instructions, which he cannot stop to see carried out, and returns into the station, where he presents his bill for travelling allowance, at the rate of eight anas a mile If there were only simple returns, such as the Magistrate himself could keep, without the assistance of a trained accountant, the engineer might be a native, who could hire for a couple of rupees an ekka or a pony that would take him to the remotest part of the district, where he could spend a day or two in the leisurely inspection of work, finding all the accommodation he required in some neighbouring village. His pay also would be counted by tens of rupees instead of by hundreds; and, as his supervision would be more continuous, there would be more of day-labour and less necessity for the employment of contractors, middle-men and munshis. These are the only people who profit by the high rates which prevail in the Department of Public Works. If the money went to the bricklayer, the mason, or the carpenter, there would be less cause for regret ; but the whole present system seems to have been invented solely for the benefit of that very unprofitable person, the artificial product of our mistaken school policy, the Munshi, the parasite of the real working community If the position of the latter were improved and their work recognised at its proper value, as in England, the son of a skilled artizan would not think to better himself, as now unfortunately he often does, by abandoning his hereditary occupation and becoming a quill-driver in an office.

The disbandment of the whole corps of executive and assistant engineers would not only be the greatest possible boon to the districts, but would even be welcomed by themselves, if due regard were had to vested interests and appointments of equal emolument found for them in a more appropriate sphere. The officers of the Roads and Building Department are the one body of Government servants in the country who notoriously have no heart in their work. It is impossible that they should have. Though by profession engineers, they are in fact merely accountants' clerks. Of all the multitudinous circulars that year by year are issued for their guidance, scarcely one per cent. refers to matters of construction. The rest are complicated rules of procedure as to filling in returns ; corrections of misprints or explanations of unintelligible phraseology in previous orders ; or most frequently of all, fulminations of the direst penalties against any attempt to exercise independent judgment. The one exception is probably either puerile or mischievous ; such as an elaborate specification and sketch of a child's tub, that was circulated not very long ago, with a sharp metal edge to it, which might be warranted to draw blood whenever used.

Again, what little work a District Engineer has to do out of his office, is profoundly uninteresting. The maintenance of a road is a task that requires no great intellect or skill, and in England would be entrusted to quite a subordinate ; while in the matter of buildings, there is no scope for the exercise of taste or ingenuity, standard plans having been provided, from which no deviation is allowed, whatever may be the differences in the locality and nature of the site. The consideration of such particulars is of less importance than might at first be imagined ; for the designs have been so skilfully contrived as to be equally unsuitable wherever they may be placed. For a man with the slightest element of humanity and good taste in his composition, it must be unspeakable misery to superintend the construction of edifices which will not only cause daily discomfort to the unfortunate officials who are doomed to use them, but will also permanently disfigure the landscape and pervert the indigenous sentiment of architectural propriety. The only innocent and legitimate source of gratification, of which the circumstances admit, lies in totalling up the number of miles for which travelling allowance can be drawn. On the other hand, no more devoted body of public servants exists than the Engineers in the Canal Department. They are taken from precisely the same class of men as their brethren on the roads ; but they are less hampered by accounts ; in dealing with such a subtle element as water, they are constantly confronted by unforeseen complications which afford exercise for ingenuity ; and they have something in which they can take an honest pride, if at the end of each successive year their returns show a larger area to which they have extended the blessings of irrigation.

In a district like Bulandshahr, with many rich, liberal, and fairly well educated members of the native aristocracy, not gathered together in a few large towns, but residing on their own estates in all parts of the country, it would be an easy matter to constitute an influential and really representative Committee for the administration of local interests. As yet, however, no tendency whatever has been shown towards decentralising the control of local finance. On the contrary, the fatal demoralisation of the whole system of local responsibility as initiated by Sir William Muir in 1871 has been still more intensified. The Examiner of Accounts in the Public Works Department is now more despotic than ever. He is allowed to sequester local subscriptions and to mete them out as grudgingly as if they were Government grants ; estimates and specifications, plans and sections, vouchers and receipts, are rigorously demanded before the pettiest work or the most trifling payment is sanctioned ; cheap day labour is disallowed, and a wasteful system of contracts enforced, as easier of record in the central bureau: in short, economy, efficiency, local convenience, and actual results are counted as nothing in comparison with the symmetry of the paper returns. So long as a committee has no definite sources of income and no independent control over them, it is an abuse of language to speak of self-government at all. What is further required is less technicality in returns and closer inspection of results. If a committee were fully trusted with the expenditure of its funds, and at the end of each year received praise for success and censure for failure, it would soon take interest in the performance of its duties. Instead of an Examiner of Accounts there would be appointed an Examiner of Works. At present it is only the accounts that are tested, and as these are far too technical for the native members of the committee to understand, their action never comes under review at all. If a work is carried out promptly and successfully, the committee gets no credit for it, but on the contrary is probably reprimanded as *troublesome*, for anticipating some purely frivolous routine formality, or for some such irregularity as failing to obtain a receipt for four or five anas from a carpenter or bricklayer on account of a day's wages. To use the emphatic words of the Provincial Committee on Education, the powers that ought to be enjoyed by local boards are "usurped by an arbitrary and overbearing department, at a great sacrifice of economy, and with the worst possible results to local convenience and progress." Nothing could be more pitiably unreal than the Committee actually existing. It is supposed to have at its disposal an annual income of over Rs. 70,000; but almost the whole of this considerable sum is absorbed by fixed charges, or has to be expended by departmental agency. A single item of about Rs. 3,000 for petty original works is all that the Committee can call absolutely its own, and can spend on projects of its own selection. If in any year this item is omitted from the budget, the Committee is then debarred from any the slightest exercise of independent judgment. Being entirely supported by arbitrary allotments, it gains nothing by judicious management; for whatever may be so realized, is merged in Provincial funds, and no benefit accrues to the district. With resources of its own, a more complete control over a less extended area, and a system of accounts which it could understand, the Committee would rapidly develope into a genuine district council, a seat in which would be highly coveted, not only as a personal distinction, but for the substantial responsibilities that it involved. The sense of local power would act as a strong stimulus to local usefulness, and spontaneous beneficial enterprise would relieve the State of many burdens now unfairly forced upon it. No reasonable person will voluntarily drop his money into the bottomless pit of a Government department, the mouth of which is so barred by checks and counterchecks that extrication can only be effected by much technical dexterity, and after the endurance of long delay. For example, a local subscription was raised in 1864 to build the English school. Only part of the money was expended at the time and the balance was invested in the 4 per cents. Twenty years later, an additional class-room becomes necessary. The Committee naturally propose to provide funds for the purpose by selling out part of their Government stock. The Collector communicates this proposal to the Commissioner at the head of the Division; and he, after recording his opinion, sends it on to the Director of Public Instruction at Naini Tal, who forwards it with a recommendation to the Secretary to Government. Sanction is thereupon accorded, which is conveyed through the same circuitous channel to the Committee. Their Secretary then applies to the Accountant General at Allahabád. The latter writes to the Comptroller General at Calcutta, who eventually remits the money to the district to which it belongs. It must be borne in mind that the particular fund in question is in no sense Government property, but belongs solely and exclusively to the local Committee, which had originally raised it by their own efforts for the identical purpose on which they now desire to employ it. But even so, it is not allowed to be kept in the Treasury as a simple deposit, but has to be credited to the Public Works accounts and must be drawn in instalments, each of which requires a formal application and has to be verified by numerous signatures and vouchers, all of which are sent for scrutiny to Allahabad. In this particular case, the procedure, cumbrous as it is, is yet comparatively simple. It involves an inevitable delay of some months, but is otherwise free from serious complications. When, however, the consent of more than one department has to be obtained, before local action can be commenced, the worry to be undergone is immensely increased. If the committee had greater freedom, it would soon acquire the confidence of the public, and become the ordinary channel for the distribution of the many streams of private benevolence, which are now too often wasted for want of effective direction.

It is one of the most convincing proofs of the general incapacity for self-government, that in many towns and villages, accumulated funds are often left unutilized, and local improvements—that every one desires—are unexecuted, simply on account of jealousy and a want of mutual confidence. If the district officer will take upon himself the responsibility of administration, the community is only too glad to place the money at his disposal and to supplement it by further subscriptions. They will not trust it to any one of themselves; and if the new road, or tank, or market-place, or whatever it may be, involves, as it generally will, the demolition of a house or two and the appropriation of the site, the owners will resist to the utmost of their power any requisition advanced by their neighbours, but will at once, and in a most liberal spirit, fall in with the wishes of a European officer. It is not that any compulsion is used, for complaint would be immediately entertained in the Civil Court, but they have confidence in their rulers, and believe them to act from more impersonal and disinterested motives than they attribute to their own townsmen.

If used as a supplement and an incentive to private enterprise and benevolence, the surplus funds of the Municipalities and Act XX.* towns might be made far more generally beneficial than they ordinarily are. During the last five years the improvements that have been effected in all the principal towns of this district are so enormous, that every visitor enquires with amazement where the money has come from. The mystery is partly explained by the larger income derived from reproductive improvements. Thus for the year ending the 30th September 1878, which was my first year in the district, the 'Miscellaneous' income of all the Act XX. towns amounted only to Rs. 572. It is now Rs. 4,900, *i. e.* nearly nine times as much. Similarly, in the Khurja Municipality the annual rent of the town lands has risen in the same period from Rs. 1,160 to Rs. 1,850, and in Bulandshahr from Rs. 507 to Rs. 1,550. If the same systematic development were maintained for another decade or two, it would then be possible in many places to abolish both the octroi and the house tax, and still have a sufficient income for local requirements. But, in order to ensure such results local knowledge is indispensable. When a Collector is simply a bird of passage, six months here and six months there, and with no special interests any where, beneficial action on his part is simply impossible, and without his initiation nothing will be done; an Indian district—like the whole of the great Oriental world—is absolutely incapable of making progress by itself. Again, the actual outlay has been much below

---

* These are a sort of second-class Municipality, constituted by Act XX of 1856, under the provisions of which a small house-tax is levied to defray the expenses of special watch and ward and of conservancy, any balance over being available for roads and drains and other such works. The income is, or can be, supplemented by market dues, slaughter-house fees, and the sale of the street sweepings for manure.

the ordinary estimate for works of such magnitude, having been reduced by a system of immediate supervision, with no contractors and middle men, and no large establishment for the elaboration of accounts and returns. But the great secret lies in the persistent adoption of the principle, that no public improvement should be undertaken unless voluntary subscriptions are forthcoming as well as State aid. In order for this system to succeed, it is necessary to be in sympathetic accord with the people, and not to force upon them anything opposed to their prejudices, or greatly in advance of their real requirements. Though themselves illiterate and indifferent to the laws of hygiene, they are quite sensible of the value of education for their children and of the advantages to be derived from bridged and avenued roads, convenient tanks and ghats for bathing purposes, good wells, clean paved streets, commodious market-places, and substantial water-tight houses. In all such works as these, the majority of the people concerned are always ready to co-operate, and even the obstructive minority will in the end be gratified by the result. Instead of the impracticable dream of purely native self-government, if only a modest scheme of decentralization were introduced, every District Committee, without the worry and delay of repeated references for sanction to higher authority, would have certain limited funds of its own to lay out in the furtherance of local projects and the encouragement of native enterprise. The result would be a great and immediate saving in State expenditure, and the eventual development of a public spirit, which would be a real qualification for higher political responsibilities.

CHAPTER II.

HISTORY OF THE TOWN OF BULANDSHAHR, FROM ITS FOUNDATION TO THE MUTINY OF 1857 A. D.

In 1824, when the present district of Bulandshahr was first formed, the town bearing that name was selected for its capital, chiefly on account of its very convenient and central situation.

Though a place of immemorial antiquity, it had fallen into decay centuries ago and had ultimately dwindled down into a miserably mean and half-deserted village. A ragged and precipitous hill, on the western bank of the narrow winding stream of the Kálindi, was all that remained of the old Fort, or rather of the succession of Forts, that in the course of 3000 years had been built, each on the accumulated debris of its predecessor. On its summit was an unfinished mosque, commenced by Sábit Khán, the Governor of Kol, in 1730, and huddled about it were some fairly large, but mostly ruinous, brick houses, occupied by the impoverished descendants of the old proprietory community and of local Muhammadan officials, such as the Kázi and the Kánungo. The rest of the population consisted of a small colony of agricultural labourers, scavengers and other menial tribes, who had squatted in their mud huts at the foot and to the west of the hill, where low mounds and ridges of broken bricks and pot-sherds, the vestiges of former habitation, alternated with swamps and ravines that collected the drainage of all the surrounding country and passed it on to the river.

Only sixty years have since elapsed and out of such unpromising materials there has now been developed as bright, cleanly and thriving a little town as can be found anywhere in the Province. The population has increased to upwards of 17,000, but it is still of much less commercial importance than the flourishing mart of Khurjá, which is only ten miles to the south and has the further advantage of possessing a station of its own on the main line of the East Indian Railway. It is, however, a matter for congratulation that in determining the site for the head quarters of the district the larger town was not given the preference; for in point of sanitation there is no comparison between the two places, Bulandshahr by reason of its raised position and consequent facilities for drainage being as healthy as Khurjá is notoriously the reverse.

The only ground for regret is that when the old historical site was adopted, the old historical name of Baran was not also restored. Bulandshahr, which—in English characters especially—has a most cumbrous and barbaric appearance, has no literary authority. Apparently it was imposed by the Muhammadans during the reign of Aurangzeb, when the ruling power was possessed with a mania—like the modern French—for the abolition of every name that suggested recollections of an earlier dynasty. In large towns, such as Mathurá and Brindaban, where also the experiment was tried, the popular appellation was too strongly rooted in the affections of the people to admit of suppression by imperial edict; but in a little place like Baran, where too the majority of the inhabitants happened to be Muhammadans, there was no difficulty in giving effect to the official innovation. The most favourable opportunity for reviving the older and shorter name has unfortunately been lost, but even now the change might be effected without causing more than a very slight and merely temporary inconvenience; for the name Baran is still perfectly familiar to the people and even officially it continues to be used as the designation both of the Pargana (or Hundred) and also of the parish, which is a very extensive one; the title Bulandshahr being applied exclusively to the town, and originally only to the Upper Town, or Fort. In meaning, it corresponds precisely with the English 'Higham,' and was suggested by the great elevation of the Castle Hill, which far overtops any other ground for many miles away. It is said by some to have been merely an Urdu rendering of the Hindi Uncha-nagar, a form that had already come into use and would bear the same signification; but, in the absence of any documentary proof of this assertion, I very strongly doubt whether the Hindus under the Delhi Emperors ever knew the place by any other name than that of Baran. There would seem to be no reason why they should substitute one indigenous name for another; while the object that the Muhammadans had, in introducing a name from their own vocabulary, is easily intelligible.

Tradition goes that in prehistoric times the town was called Banchhati—which would mean 'a forest-clearing'—and that it was founded by a Tomar, or Páṇḍava chief from Ahár, named Parmál. The site of this original settlement is the high ground now occupied by the Collector's House and the new Town Hall, and lies immediately to the west of the modern town. The spot used to be known as the 'Moti Chauk,' or 'Moti

Bazár,' meaning of course not a market where 'pearls' (*moti*) were sold, but simply a 'handsome' bazar, as we might say in English, 'a gem of a place.' The large original mound has for many years been intersected by the high road, and was also cut up by a broad and deep ravine. This latter ran down through the town to the river and was a great nuisance. I have now turned back the drainage into a tank called the 'Lál Diggi,' further to the west, near the Magistrate's Court, the overflow from which is carried by a cutting through the fields into the river higher up in its course.

In order to fill up the old ravine I levelled the ridge on its bank and, having enclosed the entire area as an adjunct to the Town Hall, am now converting it into a public garden, which—to perpetuate the old tradition—I have designated the 'Moti Bágh.' There is much vague talk of coins and solid bars of silver discovered there in former years, but in the course of my excavations I came upon nothing of much intrinsic value. Abundant proofs were, however, afforded of the interesting fact that in old times it had been occupied by Buddhists. Among my discoveries were several specimens of the curious plain stone stools, such as are figured in Plate III of Vol. XV of the Archæological Survey. General Cunningham says they are found of the same general pattern from Taxila to Palibothra and only at Buddhist sites. They were all about 6 inches high, and a foot long; but not one was unbroken. The ground had been so often disturbed before, that it was not possible to trace any definite line of building, but the fragments of walls and pavements yielded an enormous number of large and well-burnt bricks, each measuring as much as a cubit in length by half a cubit in breadth and three inches in thickness. They were mostly marked on one side by two parallel lines drawn by the workman's finger in the damp clay. Many were broken in digging them out, but many also had been laid in a broken state, as was evident from the appearance of the fracture.

Of more exceptional interest were the remains of what would seem to have been a special local manufacture, being some scores of strange earthen-ware flask or vase-like objects. They are all alike in general shape which resembles that of a cocoanut, or fir-cone, one end being pointed like a Roman amphora, with a very small orifice at the other for a mouth. But they vary very much in the patterns with which they have been ornamented, and are of different size, weight and thickness. Some apparently had been squeezed out of shape, before the material of which they were made had had time to dry. The spot where they were found is evidently that where they were baked; for, besides the failures, there was also a large accumulation of broken pieces, all mixed in a deep deposit of ashes and the other refuse of a potter's kiln.

Most natives who have seen them think they were meant to hold either gunpowder or oil, which is what the shape suggests; but the material, on account of its weight, seems unsuitable for such a purpose, if the flask was to be carried about on the person; while the pointed bottom makes it awkward for storing. The idea has also been hazarded that they were meant to be filled with gunpowder and then exploded as a kind of fire-work; but, if this were their object, there would scarcely have been so much trouble spent on their ornamentation. A third theory, which has found much favour on the spot, but which at the time I was inclined to reject as altogether untenable, is that they were intended to form a balustrade for a balcony or the roof of a house. At first my own impression was that they were not at all likely to be of the same age as the bricks. The site might have been originally occupied by a fort or a monastery and then deserted for centuries before the potters came and set up their kilns on it, making use—for their houses and workshops—of any old building-materials they happened to light upon. But finally I came to the conclusion that the balustrade theory was not so very far wrong, and that these curious objects were manufactured in such numbers in order to serve as finials for miniature Buddhist stupas. The dedication of such votive memorials was a recognized duty on a pilgrimage, and it would obviously be a convenience for worshippers to have an establishment for their manufacture and sale in immediate connection with the shrine. This view is strongly confirmed by the discovery on the same spot of what is unmistakeably a finial. It is of similar configuration and has a similar orifice at one end, which in this case is clearly intended for the admission of a supporting rod. But later again I found a *circular* flask which is of the same material and of equal weight and is ornamented in exactly the same style. It is, however, easy to grasp in the hand, and apparently was intended to hold oil or some similar fluid, for pouring out drop by drop. Thus the only definite conclusion at which it is safe to arrive is that various articles for different uses were turned out at the same factory, all being characterized by ornamentation of a peculiar local pattern.

I sent one of these objects, through a friend in England, to the British Museum, where it was considered so curious that I was asked to supply some more. Others were exhibited at a meeting of the Asiatic Society of Bengal and were afterwards transferred to the Indian Museum in Calcutta. In his valuable Catalogue of the Archæological Collections in his charge, recently published, Dr. Anderson, the Superintendent of the Museum, quotes the following note from "Nasmyth's Autobiography," which suggests that these coniferous finials were borrowed from the Greeks:—

"In conection with the worship of the Sun and other heavenly bodies as practised in ancient times by Eastern nations, it may be mentioned that their want of knowledge of the vast distances that separate them from the earth led them to the belief that these bodies were so near as to exert a direct influence upon man and his affairs. Hence the origin of Astrology, with all its accompanying mystifications; this was practised under the impression that the Sun, Moon and Planets were near to the earth. The summits of mountains and "High Places" became sacred, and were for this reason resorted to for the performance of the most important religious ceremonies.

"As the High Places could not be transported to the Temples, the cone-bearing trees, which were naturally associated with these elevated places, in a manner partook of their sacred character, and the fruit of the trees became in like manner sacred. Hence the fir-cone became a portable emblem of their sacredness; and accordingly in the Assyrian worship, so clearly represented to us in the Assyrian sculptures in our Museums, we find the fir-cone being presented by the priests towards the head of their kings as a function of beatification. So sacred was the fir-cone, as the fruit of the sacred tree, that the priest who presents it has a reticule-shaped bag, in which, no doubt, the sacred emblem was reverently deposited when not in use for the performance of these high religious ceremonies.

"The same emblem 'survived' in the Greek worship. The fir-cone was the finial to the staff of office of the Wine-god Bacchus. To this day it is employed to stir the juice of the grape previous to fermentation, and so sanctify it by contact with the fruit of the Sacred Tree. This is still practised by the Greeks in Asia Minor and in Greece, though introduced in times of remote antiquity. The fir-cone communicates to most of the Greek wines that peculiar turpentine or resinous flavour which is found in them. Although the sanctification motive has departed, the resinous flavour is all that survives of a once most sacred ceremony, as having so close a relation to the worship of the Sun and the heavenly bodies."

Most fortunately the presiding genius of the shrine where the finials were found, has also been revealed. The sculpture was dug up some twenty years ago and since then had been kept in an adjoining garden; but several people distinctly remember its being found on the same spot where the recent excavations have been made. The stone is a square block measuring in its mutilated state 1 foot 4½ inches either way, the material being a black trap, not the *sang-músa*, or black marble, of Jaypur. The principal figure represents the Buddha, enveloped in a thin robe reaching to the wrists and ankles and falling over the body in a succession of narrow folds. His arms are slightly raised in front of his breast, and the thumb and forefinger of his left hand are joined at the tips, while with his right hand he touches its middle finger, as if summing up the points of an argument. On either side of his throne is a rampant hippogriff, with its back to the sage and rearing its head over a devotee seated in an attitude of prayer. The throne is supported on two recumbent lions, flanked by Hindu caryatides with impossibly distorted limbs as usual; and at the base again are other devotees kneeling on either side of the footstool, the front of which is carved with the mystic wheel between two couchant deer. The upper part of the stone has been broken off, carrying with it the head of the principal figure, but what remains is in good preservation and has been well executed. On a ledge in a line with the feet is an inscription in characters apparently of the 9th or 10th century, which reads as follows:

Ye dharmmá hetu-prabhavá hetus teshán tathágato hyavadat teshám cha yo nirodha, evam-vádi mahásramanah.

This would be in English "All things that proceed from a cause, their cause as well as their destruction the Tathágata has declared: such is the dictum of the great philosopher." It is curious that a popular symbol of faith should have been framed with so much tautology in so short a compass, and also with such inadequacy of expression. For the cardinal feature of the doctrine, *viz.*, that effects can only be destroyed by destroying their causes, is not stated at all but merely implied.

Another very curious find was a terra cotta seal probably some 1400 years old, but as fresh and clear as if it had been baked only yesterday, and still showing the pressure of the workman's fingers who had handled the clay while it was yet damp. It was inside a closed earthen jar, which accounts for its excellent preservation. It is oval in shape, with a dotted rim, and is divided by two parallel lines across the centre into two equal compartments. In the upper are two devices, one of which is a conch shell, the other—which is raised on a little stand—looks like a wing, and may possibly be intended to represent the *chakwá*, or Bráhmani duck, so frequently introduced in old Indian painting and sculpture. In the lower compartment is the name 'Mattila,* in characters of about the 5th century A. D.

It is quite possible that the Fort on the river-bank may also have been founded by Parmál, for the protection of his infant town of Banchhati. Tradition, however, ascribes it to one of his successors, who is made to bear the name of Ahi-baran, interpreted to mean 'cobra-coloured.' But this appears to me to be absolutely untenable. Baran is certainly not the Sanskrit word *varna*, 'colour,' but *varana*, 'a hill-fort or enclosure;' and, Ahi-baran would thus mean 'snake-fort' or 'Nága fort,' in the same way as Ahi-kshetra means 'Snake-land.' No Rája Ahi-baran, I should conjecture, ever existed, though there may well have been an Ahibaran Rája, the town being so called because it was a stronghold of the Nága tribe. Nor is it impossible that the epithet 'Nága,' like the English 'reptile,' may have been attached to a Buddhist community by their Brahmanical neighbours by way of reproach. Another explanation may, however, be suggested. Some twenty-one miles to the north-east of Bulandshahr, on the right bank of the Ganges, is the small town of Ahár, which (according to local tradition) is the spot where, after Paríkshit, the successor of Rájá Yudhishthir on the throne of Hastinápur, had met his death by snake-bite, his son Janamejaya, to avenge his father's death, performed a sacrifice for the destruction of the whole serpent race. Though still accounted the capital of a Pargana, it is a miserably poor and decayed place with a population, according to the last census, of only 2,414. It is evidently, however, a site of great antiquity. Part of it has been washed away by the river, but heaps of brick and other traces of ruin still extend over a large area, and I found lying about in the streets several fragments of stone sculpture of early date. These I brought away with me to Bulandshahr, as also a once fine but now terribly mutilated round pillar, which I dug up on the

* Dr. Hœrnle has suggested to me that it might be read 'Hattiya.'

very verge of the high cliff overlooking the river. This is specially noticeable as having its base encircled with a coil of serpents, which would seem to corroborate the connection of the local name with the word *ahi*, 'a snake.' The principal residents of the town are Nágar Bráhmans by descent, though—since the time of Aurangzeb—Muhammadans by religion, who believe that their ancestors were the priests employed by Janamejaya to conduct his sacrifice, and that in return for their services they had a grant of the township and the surrounding villages. Immediately after this event it is said that the Páṇḍavas transferred their seat of local government from Ahár to Baran, and it may be that they then first attached the prefix *ahi* to the name of the town—so making it Ahibaran—in order to commemorate the circumstances of the migration. This would imply that the town was already in existence; and it might with much plausibility be identified with the Váranávata,* mentioned in the 143rd chapter of the first Book of the Mahábhárat,

All this, however, is conjectural and refers to a period so remote, nearly 1400 years before Christ, that no tangible record of it could be expected to survive to the present day. To come down to somewhat later times: the Bactrian dynasty, which flourished in the centuries immediately preceding our era, and the Gupta dynasty that succeeded it, have both left traces behind them. In the rains, copper and gold coins with Greek and Páli inscriptions, used so frequently to be washed down in the debris from the high ground of the old town, at a particular point, now called 'the Manihárs' or bangle-makers' quarter,' that after any heavy storm people made it a regular business to search for them. To prevent further cutting away, the slope was built up with masonry in 1876; but even since then two copper coins of Su-Hermæus, styled Basileus Soter, a gold coin of Chandra Gupta II, and another of an intermediate dynasty, have been picked up, which I presented to the coin cabinet of the Asiatic Society of Bengal.

It may thus be concluded that the town of Baran at the commencement of the Christian era was a place of some wealth and importance;

---

* General Cunningham proposes to identify with the Váranávata of the Mahábhárata a village, now called Barnáwa, in the Merath district. It has not yet been explored, and it is therefore uncertain whether it is really an ancient site or not.

while the discovery of the antiquities above described clearly establishes the interesting fact that a little later, from about 400 to 800 A. D., there was a Buddhist community outside the Fort walls, occupying the site now known as the Moti Bágh. The only ancient inscriptions that have been found in the district are distinctly Brahmanical. The oldest is dated in the reign of Skanda Gupta, in the year 146, which—if the Saka era in intended—would correspond with 224 A. D. But this dynasty had an era of its own, which seems more likely to have been the one used, and an element of considerable uncertainty is thus introduced. For the commencement of the Gupta era is a very *vexata quæstio* among archæologists, being put by some so late as 319 A. D., by others at 190, and now by Gen. Cunningham at 167. A complete transcript and translation of the inscription, by Dr. Rájendralála Mitra, C. I. E., are given in Vol. XLIII of the Journal of the Asiatic Society of Bengal. It is not in itself of great importance, being simply a provision on the part of a Bráhman, named Deva-vishṇu, for the maintenance of an oil lamp, to burn in a temple of the Sun at Indra-pura. The copper-plate on which it is engraved was dug up at Indor, an artificial mound of great elevation and extent, a little off the high road from Anúpshahr to Aligarh, opposite the eighth mile-stone from the former town. As I have shewn at length in my "Mathurá," by an application of the rules laid down by the Prákrit grammarian Vararuchi, the Sanskrit Indra-pura, in the natural course of phonetic decay, must become Indor in the modern vernacular. Besides the inscription, a large number of coins, some of an older type than those of the Asoka period, together with beads, fragments of terra cotta, brass ornaments, toys and other trifles were found by Mr. Carlleyle, during his exploration of the mound. The most unimportant of them were presented to the Indian Museum; the remainder, it is presumed, are in General Cunningham's possession.

The next inscribed memorial is some centuries later in date, but from exposure to rough usage is in a far less perfect state of preservation and is for the most part illegible. It is an oblong block of stone, measuring 29 inches by 10 by 10, which I brought into the station from the well adjoining the tomb of Khwája Lál Barani, which lies across the Kálindi, and close by the side of the Shikárpur road, about half a mile due east of the town of Bulandshahr.* There are two inscriptions, one opposite the other,

---

* This historical site had been for many years in a very neglected condition. It is

in characters of different size, but of the same period, probably about 1200 A. D. Both are records of grants for religious purposes, and the stone must have been intended for deposit among the archives of the temple for which the endowments were provided. But it can never have been actually set up, as it is difficult to imagine a position in which both sides could be conveniently read; it is also evident that preparations had been made for splitting it up into two separate slabs of equal thickness. One of the two inscriptions opens with an invocation of Krishna, in the words *Om Namo Bhagavate Vásudeváya.* I have had it deposited, in the Indian Museum, Calcutta.

Of far greater significance is a copper-plate inscription, which was dug up in 1867 at the village of Mánpur, in the Agota Pargana, about eight miles to the north of the town of Bulandshahr. Natives, even of the higher and more educated classes, have a childish notion, of which it is quite impossible to disabuse them, that these old copper-plate inscriptions always refer to some buried treasure. Thus the Council of the Mahárája of Jaypur, on hearing of the Mánpur find, at once put in a claim for anything of value that might be discovered; on the plea that Mánpur had been founded by Rája Mán Siñh of the Jaypur line. The absurdity of the claim was in this case enhanced by the confusion of chronological ideas; for Mán Siñh was a contemporary of Akbar's, while the plate is anterior to the reign of Prithi Ráj. It was sent to the Asiatic Society in Calcutta, and a translation of it into Nágari and English by Pandit Pratápa Chandra Ghosh, appeared in Vol. XXXVIII of the Journal of the Calcutta Asiatic Society. By a strange fatality, the three most important words in the whole record, *viz.*, those which give the name of the reigning family, the name of the country, and the century of the date, are the most doubtful and illegible. The year—which is written at full length, in words—ends with 'thirty-three,' but the initial letters have been obliterated by rust. The century, however, must be either the eleventh or twelfth, for the characters belong to the period immediately succeeding that of the Kutila inscriptions. The date may thus be confidently accepted as either 1133 or 1233 *Samvat, i. e.*, either 1076 or 1176 of the Christian era. The earlier of the two seems the more probable.

---

now being enclosed with an ornamental brick wall at a cost of about Rs. 1000 contributed by the Muhammadan residents of the town.

The grant—which confers a village named Gandavá on a certain Gaur Bráhman—was made by a Rája Ananga, in whose description a word occurs which the Calcutta Pandit first took to be 'Kalinga.' But the only country so-called is an extensive tract far away on the sea-coast, south of Bengal. It was never owned by a single sovereign—which in itself creates a difficulty—and it is further inconceivable how a plate relating to so distant a region could have found its way into the Doáb. The word is very indistinct and ambiguous and (as the Pandit has remarked) may with equal probability be read *kanishṭha*, which will also give an intelligible sense to the passage. The suggestion of 'Kalinga' seems therefore to have been an unnecessary importation of a somewhat gratuitous difficulty. It might perhaps be *Koláusa*. This is given in Monier Williams's Dictionary as the name of a district, placed by some in Gangetic Hindustán, with Kanauj for its capital, but which it would seem more natural to identify with the country round about Kol, the modern Aligarh.

The name of the family was read by the Pandit as 'Rodra'; but only with great hesitation, and with the admission that it seemed to be something different, though he could not exactly say what. It is really Ḍoṛ, the name of an almost extinct Rájput tribe, who once were very notable people in these parts, though a Sanskrit scholar in Bengal may well be pardoned for not remembering them. They claim to be a branch of the great Pramár clan, which in ancient times was the most powerful of all the Rájput tribes; "The world is the Pṛamár's" being quoted by Col. Tod as a proverbial saying to illustrate their extensive sway. They represent their ancestor to have been a Pramár Rája of Mainpuri, who cut off his own head for a sacrifice to the divinity; whence his descendants were styled Ḍunḍ, 'the headless,' afterwards corrupted into Ḍoṛ. But this is obviously a mere etymological fable. Chand in the Prithiráj-Rásá celebrates a Ḍoṛ chief of Kasondi, a locality which cannot now be identified with certainty, though probably it was a place that still bears the same name near Ajmer. The Ḍoṛs are also mentioned in a Sanskrit inscription of the time of Prithiráj, which was found by Colonel Skinner at Hánsi. This forms the basis for a rhapsody by Col. Tod in his usual enthusiastic vein, which is published in Vol. I of the Transactions of the Royal Asiatic Society. In the body of the article the tablet is described as commemorating a victory obtained over the Ḍoṛs; but what purports to be a more or less literal summary of the inscription is given at the end of the narrative, and all that can be gathered from this is, that in the course of the concluding stanzas the Ḍoṛs are mentioned, but in what character, whether as foes or allies, does not appear. The summary unfortunately is most inadequate; but the main object of the inscription would seem to have been to record the date not of any victory, but of the extension of a fort at Ásí, which presumably was the older name of Hánsi. This work is said to have been executed by a General named Hammíra in conjunction with the Gahlot chief Kilhana, who is described—in Tod's translation—as Prithiráj's maternal uncle. But here lies a difficulty; for Prithiráj's mother was Kamala-Devi, one of the daughters of King Anangpál, who was a Tomar not a Gahlot, and who had no male issue. The date of this Hánsi inscription is *Sambat* 1224 (1168 A. D.). It was found in 1818 and presented to Lord Hastings; but in 1824, the date of Tod's article, it was not known what had become of it. In fact, a singular fatality seems to attend all the records of this ancient Hindu clan—once so considerable, now virtually extinct—for I find, on enquiry in Calcutta, that the Mánpur inscription also has disappeared and cannot be traced.

This grant enumerates fourteen successive Rájas, beginning with Chandraka, the founder of the particular family. The seventh in descent was Haradatta, who was succeeded first by his brother, secondly by a nephew, and only in the third place by his son, who was subsequently deposed by a Bráhman minister, who both secured the throne for himself and bequeathed it to his son. The parentage of the thirteenth Rája is not distinctly stated, as it is in every other case, and hence it may be surmised that he was not related to his immediate predecessor, but belonged to the original Ḍoṛ stock. This is the more probable, because if he and his son Ananga had been descendants of the Bráhman usurper, the introduction of the Ḍoṛ pedigree would be altogether out of place.

The names stand as follows:

1. Chandraka.
2. Dharaṇi-varáha.
3. Prabhása.
4. Bhairava.
5. Rudra

6. Govinda-rája (surnamed Yasopara).

7. Hara-datta. — 8. Bhogáditya — (unnamed)

10. Vikramáditya (son of 7). — 9. Srikuláditya (son of the unnamed one).

11. Bhúpati, surnamed Padmáditya, Bráhman Minister.

12. Bhojadeva.

13. Sahajáditya.

14. Ananga.

The above genealogy is of very exceptional interest, because it is known from other sources that at the time of the invasion of India by Mahmúd of Ghazni in 1017 A. D., Merath, Baran and Kol were all held by the Ḍors and that Har-datt was the name of their Rája, who had his principal residence at Baran. He is mentioned as follows by the Muhamadan Chronographer: "When the Sultan marched on the fortress of Merath, its Raja, who bore the name of Hardatt,* made it over to trusty persons and himself left it for another part of his dominions (probably Baran). The garrison perceived that they had no power of resistance, so they offered as a tribute 1,000,000,000 darhams, which amount to Rs. 2,50,000, and 30 elephants and obtained terms." His cowardly flight and the disgrace that he thus incurred may very probably be the explanation of the fact briefly stated in the Mánpur inscription that his son was twice passed over in the succession to the throne and was eventually deposed.

Before these events there is reason to conclude that Har-datt was the most important chief in all this part of the country between Kanauj and Thanesar. For Delhi, though refounded by the Rája Dháva of the Iron Pillar about 319 A. D. and again rebuilt in 731 by Anang Pál, the first Tomar Rája of that name, is not once mentioned either by the Chinese Pilgrims or by Al Utbi, and was probably at this period a small, unfortified and quite unimportant village; the capital of the Tomars being at Kanauj. When that city was taken by Chandra Deva, the founder of the

* The MSS. give the name as Harwat: in Persian characters *d* and *w* are easily interchangeable.

Rahtor dynasty, about 1050 A. D., Anang Pál II retired to Delhi and there established himself. But at the beginning of the eleventh century, Har-datt, the Rája of Baran, though nominally a feudatory of Kanauj, appears to have been the virtual sovereign of all the country now included in the districts of Aligarh, Bulandshahr, Merath and Delhi, with parts of Murádabád, Mathurá and Eta.

His name is still perpetuated by Hápur, a corruption of Hara-pur, now the head-quarters of the Stud Depôt, of which town he is the traditional founder, and all the fragments of stone sculpture that have been discovered at Bulandshahr may be assigned to his time. As might have been expected from its nearness to Delhi, the Muhammadans have made a clean sweep of the district and razed to the ground every building, secular or religious, that had been erected by its former Hindu rulers. I have been over every part of it, but the sum total of all the antiquities I have been able to collect may be very briefly enumerated. An unusually lofty column is one of a pair that were dug up in some low ground at the entrance to the town from the Chola Railway Station. Though long since brought under cultivation, the field is still called 'the Sarovar,' and is the traditional site of a large masonry 'tank' which Har-datt is said to have constructed. The companion column is at Merath, where it was sent by the Sardár Bahádur, into whose hands it had come, and has been worked up into a house he has built there. The one now in my possession I rescued from his stables, where it had been thrown on the ground and was used by his grass-cutters to sharpen their tools on. Six short pillars of the same period were found buried under the steps of a small mosque on the highest part of the old town. In digging the foundations of a house on the opposite side of the same street I recovered a curious stone, sculptured with a representation of three miniature temples. These are of such different design that, if they had been found separately, I might have been inclined to refer them to different architectural epochs. But the excessively archaic type of one must be attributed to the influence of religious conservatism ; similar forms may be seen in conjunction on the front of the temples of Khajuráho, which are known to be of the tenth century A. D. A circular pillar, with a coil of human-headed snakes at the base, is, as already mentioned, from Ahár, as also a mediæval door-jamb and a block carved with rows of temple facades in the style of the Násik caves. This last is probably the oldest of the group. Another door-jamb, found in the court-yard of the mosque at Bulandshahr, is comparatively modern.

The Sarovar, or Tank, field, of which I have spoken above, is bounded on the north by an extensive mound, on which now stands the stable for Government stallions, and in levelling part of it I came upon two curious terra cotta figures, both alike, 5¼ inches high, representing a woman with a parrot, which she is about to feed with a fruit she holds in one hand. She has enormous ornaments in her ears and a variety of chains and bracelets about her. Another fragment--a head only—shows a chignon of most prodigious dimensions. In the absence of stone, the potter's art seems to have been largely developed for decoration and religious purposes, as is further indicated by a clay statue of the four-armed Krishna, which I discovered in breaking down an old well in the upper town. The exact date of these figures cannot be determined.

The Mánpur inscription gives Vikram-áditya as the name of Haradatta's son, and he is probably the same person as a Rája Vikram Sen of Baran, who figures in an Aligarh pedigree. The capital of that branch of the Ḍoṛ family is said to have been transferred from Jaláli to Kol by Buddh Sen, who was the son of Bijay Rám (brother of Dasarath Siñh, who built the fort at Jalesar) the son of Náhar Siñh, (founder of the Sambhal Fort) the son of Gobind Siñh, who was the son of Mukund Sen, the son of Rája Vikram Sen of Baran, Mangal Sen, who succeeded his father, the above-mentioned Buddh Sen, at Kol, is said to have given his daughter Padmávaṭi in marriage to the heir of Rája Bhím of Mahrára and Etáwa, who soon after his accession was murdered by his younger brothers. The widow then returned to Kol, where her father built for her the tower, which was wantonly destroyed by the local authorities in 1860. It is, however, more commonly believed that the tower was erected by the Muhammadans in 1274 on the site of the principal Hindu temple, to commemorate the final reduction of the town in the reign of Násir-ud-dín Mahmúd. Possibly it had been built by the Rája and was only enlarged or otherwise altered by the conquerors.

Eighty years before the fall of Kol, *viz.*, in 1193, the Ḍoṛ line of Rájas at Baran had come to an end in the person of Chandra Sen, who was killed while defending his fort against the army of Shaháb-ud-dín Muhammad Ghori. Before he fell, an arrow from his bow had slain one of the leaders of the invading force, a certain Khwája Lál Ali, whose tomb across the Kálindi is still reverenced as that of a martyr.* The gate was opened to the enemy by two traitors, one a Bráhman named Híra Siñh, the other Ajaypál, himself a Ḍoṛ, who probably hoped by this act of perfidy to secure recognition as the future head of the family and the most fitting person to continue its hereditary honours. All, however, that he actually obtained from the conqueror was the subordinate post of Chauḍhari, with the sonorous title of Malik Muhammad Daráz Kadd; the latter being the reward for his profession of Islám; while the administration of the new province was conferred upon a fellow-countryman of the victorious General, Kázi Núr-ud-dín of Ghazni. The descendants of this, the first Muhammadan Governor of Baran, still occupy a respectable position in the town and retain their ancestor's title of Kázi. Similarly, Ajaypál's decendants still style themselves Chaudharis; though the name by which they are more commonly designated is Tánṭas, or Mischief-makers. These unworthy representatives of a long line of independent princes form a fairly numerous section of the community but are badly off and of ill-reputation. They are one and all Muhammadans. During the raid of the Sikhs in 1780 they opened the gate of the town to them, in imitation of their recreant forefather; and again in the Mutiny of 1857 they were the first to plunder the bazar. The social distinction of the old family has been better transmitted in the female line by a daughter of the house, who was given in marriage to the Bargújar chief Pratáp Siñh, who came up from Rájaur, now in the Jaypur State, to join Prithi Ráj of Delhi in his attack on Mahoba. After the conquest he returned no more to his own country, but settled down at Pahásu, where he is now represented by his direct descendant Nawáb Sir Faiz Ali Khán, K. C. S. I.

To sum up the Hindu Annals of Baran. It was founded about a thousand years before Christ by Tomar chiefs from Delhi: under the Indo-Scythian and Gupta dynasties, at the commencement of our era, it

---

* In order to secure a blessing on their labours, the dancing girls of the town, before entering on the regular practice of their profession, generally make a vow to perform their first dance in front of this tomb. It is largely visited by the people of the neighbourhood on the festival of the Bakr-I'd, and on that day a venerable *nim* tree, which overshadows it, is said to show forth an annual miracle, its naturally bitter leaves becoming quite sweet.

was a place of some wealth and importance; and for a considerable period, up to the ninth or tenth century, it included in its population a community of Buddhists. About the year 800 A. D. the Ḍoṛ Rájputs rose to power, and their leader Chandraka, having established himself as a Rája, made Baran his capital. His descendant in the sixth degree, Hara-datta, founded the town of Hápur and ruled an extensive tract of country including Merath and Kol; but, in 1017, being hard-pressed by Mahmúd's invading force, he submitted to terms, which lost him the confidence of his people. On the withdrawal of the conqueror, domestic disturbances ensued, but—after a temporary usurpation—the old dynasty was eventually restored and occupied the throne till the year 1193, when Rája Chandra Sen, the last of the line, was defeated and killed by the army of Kutb-ud-dín, and the Fort then passed into the hands of the Muhammadans.

Under the new administration it would seem to have been still considered a place of military importance. On the accession of Kai Kubád in 1286 A. D. Malik Tuzáki, a man of high rank and importance in Balban's reign and Muster-master General (*A'riz-i-mamálik*) held the fief of Baran; and after he had been got rid of by the favourite Nizám-ud-dín, his appointments were conferred upon Jálal-ud-dín, who in 1290 became Emperor. His murderer and successor Alá-ud-dín, also made it for some days his head-quarters before he marched upon Delhi, and it was here that he received the submission of all the principal nobles, whom he bought over from the cause of the rightful heir by a lavish distribution of the treasure that he had captured at Deogiri; the leaders receiving twenty, thirty, and some even fifty *mans* of gold, and all their soldiers 300 *tankas* each.* He is described as holding his levy in the open space before the town mosque. The present Jama Masjid was not built till 440 years later, but an earlier structure probably preceded it on the same site. This is on the verge of the hill; but in front of the main gate there is an area of considerable extent, which is fairly level, though now completely covered by a labyrinth of narrow lanes, with mud hovels reaching up to the very walls of the Mosque enclosure and even built on to the staircase, which is its only approach. As the claim for compensation cannot involve any very large outlay, I am anxious to pull down some of these miserable tenements, and

* The *tanka* is the name for the current coinage of the time, the exact value of which is uncertain. Fifty *mans* of gold would be more than 35 cwt.!

again open out a small square in front of what is the principal religious building in the place. That such encroachments should have been allowed, or rather committed, by the Muhammadan guardians of the Mosque is an illustration of the carelessness with which the citizens of an Indian town ordinarily administer their own public institutions.

The new Governor, Mayid-ul-Mulk, whom Alá-ud-din put in charge of Baran,—though of no celebrity himself—is noteworthy as the father of the only distinguished literary character that the town has produced. This was Zia-ud-dín, called Barani from the place of his birth, who wrote the history entitled 'the Chronicles of Firoz Sháh.' It is brought down to the year 1356, at which time the author was 74 years of age. His grave, according to local tradition, is at the spot called the Kálá Ám—from an old mango tree that once stood there—at the junction of the six roads near the District Courts. Every Thursday evening a cloth is spread over it and lamps are lit at its head, but there is no monument nor inscription. Indeed, it is asserted by some authorities that he was not buried at Bulandshahr at all, but at Delhi, in the Nizám-ud-dín cemetery, near his friend, the poet Amír Khusro, who died in 1325. Prof. Blochmann, a thoroughly competent critic, speaks of him as a most miserable writer, so far as style is concerned; his language being Hindi literally translated into Persian. As regards matter, however, which in an historical authority is the point of most importance, he is by no means devoid of merit. Despite his literary defects, Prof. Dowson describes him as a vigorous, plain-spoken writer, who may unhesitatingly be indicated as the one most acceptable to a general reader, and whose pages may be read without that feeling of weariness and oppression which the writings of his fellows too commonly produce. His work was intended as a continuation of the Tabakát-i-Násiri of Minháj-ud-dín Jurjáni. It contains the history of eight kings, Balban, Kai-Kubád, the three Khiljis, the two Tughlaks and Firoz Sháh. The history of the last reign, though the one which gives its title to the book, is incomplete and of less interest than the other portions, the value of the narrative being affected by a strain of excessive adulation. He is said to have died in such poverty that even a proper shroud could not be provided for his body which had to be wrapt up in a piece of coarse matting. But the truth of this tradition may be questioned; the continuer of his history expressly states that his death was greatly regretted by the Emperor, and both his father and uncle had occupied important positions at Court, the latter, Alá-ul-Mulk having been the Kotwál, or Police Magistrate, of Delhi.

In the reign of Firoz's predecessor, Muhammad Tughlak, (1325 to 1351 A. D.) the town of Baran suffered dearly for its proximity to Delhi, being one of the first places where that sanguinary tyrant diverted himself with his favourite spectacle of an unprovoked massacre In the great famine of 1344, after the removal of the Capital to Deogiri, the country of the Doáb—to use the language of the local historian—"was brought to great distress by heavy taxation and numerous cesses. The Hindus burnt their corn-stacks and turned their cattle out to roam at large. Under the orders of the Sultán the Collectors and Magistrates laid waste the country, killing some of the land-owners and village chiefs and blinding others. Such of the unhappy inhabitants as escaped formed themselves into bands and took refuge in the jungles. So the country was ruined. The Sultán then proceeded on a hunting excursion to Baran, where—under his directions—the whole of that neighbourhood was plundered and laid waste and the heads of the Hindus were brought in and hung upon the ramparts of the Baran Fort." Though it was a matter of impossibility to collect the revenue, the Hindu Governor was put to death for his failure to do so, and a vast number of his kinsmen, a Baniya clan called Baran-wálas, whose ancestors, had been settled in the town by its first founders, were driven into exile. Some of them emigrated to Murádabád, while others fled as far as Azamgarh and Gházipur, in both which districts they are now more numerously represented than in their original home.

Of those who remained at Baran, one family in the reign of Akbar acquired for themselves the post of hereditary Kánungo ; and one of their descendants, Shaikh Roshan, who was converted to Islám by the persuasive arguments of Aurangzeb, founded the suburb—as it then was—called Shaikh Saráe, which now by the increase of population has become a very central locality. Of the same stock are Munshi Shaháb-ud-dín, the builder of the large mosque, which from its lofty situation is the most conspicuous feature in any general view of the town, and the late Masúm Ali Khán of Murádabád, whose son Munawar Ali Khán, being of weak intellect, is under the charge of the Court of Wards. The handsome range of shops in the market-place, built in 1882, is part of his estate.

SHOPS IN THE MARKET PLACE
BULANDSHAHR
1882

SCALE 3 FEET TO 1 INCH

Of the Baranwálas, who adhered to the old faith, the most conspicuous person in the present century was Sítal Dás, who about the year 1830, built that portion of lower Bulandshahr which is known as Sítal Ganj, and is now the property of his son Prem-sukh Dás.

In spite of the massacre and famine and wholesale expulsion of the inhabitants that took place in 1344, Zia-ud-dín relates that his native town rapidly revived under the more benign sway of Firoz Sháh. At some time during his reign, which lasted from 1351 to 1388, that Emperor founded Khurja, which has become the largest commercial mart in the neighbourhood; a part of it is still called Firoz Ganj. More than a century later, Sikandar Lodi, about the year 1500, founded what are now the two considerable towns of Sikandarabád and Shikárpur, at which latter place—as the name indicates—he had a small hunting-box for occasional residence. The only two other towns of any size in the district, Anúpshahr and Jahángirabád, were founded later still, in the reign of Jahángir; which shows, how essentially modern the present centres of population are, excepting only Bulandshahr itself and Dibhái:* the latter is occasionally mentioned by the early Muhammadan historians as a muster-place for troops.

The prosperity which the country had enjoyed during the long and settled reign of Firoz was followed by a series of fratricidal struggles between his sons and grandsons for the possession of the throne, and then by the ruin and rapine of foreign invasion. On the capture of Delhi by the Mughals in 1398, the puppet Emperor Mahmúd fled away to Gujarát, while the Regent, Ikbál Khán, took refuge in the fort of Baran. Tímúr soon returned home with his plunder to Samarkand, and on his departure Nusrat Sháh—also one of Firoz's grandsons—marched up from Merath and reoccupied the ruins of the capital, whence he sent a large force "under Shaháb Khán to Baran to overpower Ikbál.† On the way, a band of Hindu foot-soldiers fell upon him in the night and killed him and dispersed his followers. As soon as Ikbál heard of this, and that the elephants also

* Dibhái is a corruption of the Sanskrit Darbhavati. There is an old town in the Bombay Presidency, in the territory of the Gaekwár of Baroda, which bears the same name a little differently spelt, Dabhoi, which is a somewhat closer approximation to the original form. The substitution of *i* for *a* is one of the most marked peculiarities of up-country speech.

† Tárikh i Mubárak Sháh of Yahya bin Ahmad.

had been abandoned, he hastened to the spot and secured them. From that time his power and renown increased daily, and forces gathered round him, while Nusrat Khán grew weaker and weaker, so that after a stay of ten months he was able to leave Baran and recover possession of Delhi." He also got into his hands the person of the Sultán Mahmúd, whom he afterwards took to Kanauj and left there, while he himself reigned as the real sovereign of the country, till 1405, when he fell in battle at Multán.

Two years later, *viz.*, in 1407, Ibráhim Sháh, the king of Jaunpur, marched up against Delhi, where Mahmúd was then enthroned; but hearing of disturbances at home he hastened back, leaving Marhaba Khán, a protegé of Ikbál's, with a small force, at Baran. After six months Mahmúd marched from Delhi against Baran, and Marhaba Khán came out to meet him; but in the battle that ensued he was beaten and driven back into the fort, where the Imperial troops followed and killed him.

The next mention of Baran is in 1421, during the reign of Khizr Khán, the first of the Saiyid dynasty, when the Vazir, Táj-ul-Mulk, marched through it on his way to suppress a rebellion in Kol and Etáwa. Again, in 1434, after the assassination of Khizr's successor, Mubárak Sháh, an army of the Hindu Vazír's, Sarwar-ul-Mulk, under the command of Kamál-ud-dín, proceeding against Allah Dád, the chief of the insurgents, halted at Baran, the half-way station between the Jamuná and the Ganges. Allah Dád withdrew to Ahár, where the two generals came to an understanding and turned their combined forces against the Vazír, whom they besieged in the fort of Delhi, where shortly afterwards he was slain in an attempt on the life of the Emperor Muhammad Sháh.

The earliest Persian inscription in Bulandshahr is a tablet let into the wall of the I'd-gáh, which records the construction of a mosque by Nek-bakht Khán, in the year 943 *Hijri* (1536 A. D.) in the reign of the Emperor Humáyun and during the governorship "of the chaste Báno Begam." The fact of a female Governor is somewhat curious. At Til Begampur, fifteen miles north-west of Bulandshahr, is a bathing-well (or *báoli*) with an inscription dated only two years later, *viz.*, 1538, in which the local Governor's name is given as Amír Fakír Ali Beg. As an I'd-gáh would not be styled a mosque, the stone must have been brought from elsewhere, but probably from the immediate neighbourhood. Fragments of an Arabic inscription in Cufic characters have also been inserted in the same wall at regular distances, to serve as decorative panels, and the later Persian inscription seems to have been utilized with simply the same object. The appearance of this building, with its blackened and crumbling masonry, is scarcely creditable to the Muhammadan community, who should take some steps to clean and repair it.

About 100 yards to the east of the I'd-gáh and the adjoining English cemetery, is a square-domed tomb of substantial brick masonry and some size, but no particular architectural merit, with a Persian inscription. This records its completion during the reign of the Emperor Akbar, in the year 1006 *Hijri* (1597 A. D.) as a monument to the memory of Miyán Bahlol Khán Bahádur. He belonged to the Bahlím clan of Shaikhs, and his descendants continued in possession of an extensive tract of freehold land in the suburbs, till 1857, when they forfeited it by their complicity with the mutineers. One of the outlying hamlets, included in the straggling parish of Baran, still bears the name of Bahlímpura.

At the beginning of the seventeenth century, and probably for some years later, Baran continued to be the capital of a *dastúr*, or district, in the Home Sarkár, or Division, of the Delhi Súba, or Province. But the town must have rapidly sunk into insignificance, and eventually it became a dependency of Kol. It receives no further mention in any historical record after the Ain-i-Akbari, and the only event of even local interest, that forms a landmark in the later Muhammadan period, is the foundation of the Jama Masjid in 1730. This was built by Sábit Khán, who achieved special distinction as Governor of Kol. There he is commemorated by his restoration of the old Fort, which he called Sábit-gaṛh ; by a *dargáh*, bearing date 1707 ; and still more by the great mosque in the centre of the town, which he completed in 1728. His tomb is in the garden now known as Kinloch-ganj. The Bulandshahr mosque is of much less pretension and, being unfinished at the time of his death, remained so till more than a hundred years later. His lineal descendants at Aligarh, however poor their circumstances, and most of them are mere labourers, are distinguished by the personal title of Nawáb, in remembrance of their ancestor. In Bulandshahr his success as a proselytizer is evidenced by several families—originally Thákurs of the Bargújar clan—who were led by him to adopt Muhammadanism and who have ever since borne the name of Sábit-kháni.

Fifty years later, *viz.*, in 1780, Baran had its final fall, being then abandoned even by the Amil, or subordinate revenue official, who had hitherto made it his head-quarters. The spot that he selected in preference was on the opposite side of the river, some six miles to the north. The village had previously been known as Rathora; but the new Fort was placed by its founder, the A'mil Hak-dád Khán, under the patronage of a saint, popularly styled Málamál, who had a shrine close by, and it received the name of Málagaṛh. In 1857 Hak-dád's grandson, Walidád Khán, put himself at the head of the revolt and proved a formidable opponent. He was connected with the royal family of Delhi—his sister's daughter having been married to one of the king's sons—and he had thus obtained from Muhammad Bahádur a formal grant appointing him Súbadar of this part of the Doáb. Málagaṛh became the resort of all the disaffected from far and near; his troops overran the whole neighbourhood, fought several sharp engagements, and for a few days occupied the town of Bulandshahr. On the 28th of September they were driven out, and their leader escaped across the Ganges. The demolition of his fort at Málagaṛh, which took place a few days later, was accompanied by a deplorable accident. The officer who fired the mine was Lieut. Home of the Engineers, one of the heroes of the Kashmir Gate, and he was killed by the explosion. His body was interred in the Station Cemetery, where a handsome stone monument forms a conspicuous object and records the untimely death of the first V. C. in India.

MARKET SQUARE, BULANDSHAHR.

CHAPTER III.

THE REBUILDING OF BULANDSHAHR.

THAT architecture in India is still a living art, with unlimited capabilities of healthy expansion, is an axiom that few competent and unprejudiced critics would hesitate to accept. It is true that the fact of this vitality is often confidently denied, as by a recent writer in the *Graphic*, who, "after thirty years' experience of Indian life and character," declares that "all the indigenous art we have now to admire in Hindustan is ancient art, the art of people who lived hundreds and thousands of years ago." A similar opinion is still more deliberately expressed by a contributor to the *Calcutta Review* for January 1884, whose words are as follows: "If any one doubts the fallacy of an observation that has lately been made that 'architecture is still a living art in India,' we would only ask him to travel a little in the interior with his eyes open. He will find whole architectural provinces (if the term may be applied where the art does not exist) in which every rule of work, and every sense of the fitness of things has been lost sight of. He will see Hindu temples built in a debased style of Muhammadan architecture, the debasements being so great that a further depth cannot be imagined. Or, where the proper Indo-Aryan forms have been adhered to, the superstructure will be found loaded with hideous ornamentation, in lieu of the chaste simplicity of the ancient types." Yet he goes on to say "even now a beautiful building occasionally rises up in a small district where foreign influence is away"; and this final admission virtually cancels the previous statement that the art is absolutely dead. Vitality is not extinct, but is only temporarily and accidentally suspended, and can be re-awakened. Both these critics and all who agree with them find an easy and a plausible argument for their despair of an Indian architectural revival in the undeniable hideousness of the vast majority of our modern buildings. But the induction is imperfect; it has not been sufficiently considered who are really responsible for these architectural enormities.

It is no matter for surprise that the people themselves, if questioned as to the existence and prospects of indigenous art, entirely fail to comprehend the purport of the enquiry; for, in any community, the masses are habitually as unconscious of the progress of national sentiment, as a man is of his own growth in stature. The development now actually in progress is no artificial novelty, for the importation of which a definite date can be assigned. It is rather the necessary result of an involuntary adaptation to the varying circumstances of modern life, and is the more unfelt because the laws so ceaselessly modified are oral and traditional, not written.

It is true that the Hindu *Shastras* include a series of treatises, which are professedly devoted to architecture and the other fine or mechanical arts; but manuscripts are exceedingly scarce, the text is often hopelessly corrupt, and the instructions are almost exclusively of a ritual character, concerning the selection of auspicious sites and days, and the proper location of images and altars. Hence it comes about that the only recognized standard of design is local custom, dating backwards it may be from immemorial antiquity, and thus fixed in principle, though ever varying in form with the variations of fashion and the requirements of modern civilization.

Beyond the buildings themselves, there is no record in existence of the new rules of proportion, and the foreign canons of taste, which were the necessary sequence of the Muhammadan invasion and the introduction of the arch. At Ahmadabad, in the Bombay Presidency, and at Jaunpur, in the North-West, the struggle between the old style and the new led to a singularly picturesque combination, which—despite the distance between the two cities and the absence of intercourse—in both places presents very similar features. The influences at work were precisely the same. A Muhammadan Court, at once bigoted and magnificent, was ambitious to embellish its capital and display its devotion, but was unable to carry out its ideas, except by the exclusive employment of Hindu craftsmen, of alien religion and opposite sympathies. The results, though highly interesting, are marred by the intrinsic incongruity of the component parts. This was soon felt to be a defect and was gradually toned down; but with its disappearance disappeared also the whole charm of the style, which was never more than a beautiful hybrid, doomed to early decay and with no power of reproduction.

The eclecticism of Akbar's reign was less forced in its origin, and has been more permanent in its effects, for they continue to the present day. In the three-and-a-half centuries that had elapsed since the death of the last Hindu Sovereign of Delhi, Saracenic art had become thoroughly naturalized, and its fusion with the older indigenous style was the inevitable outcome of the closer and more equal intercourse between the two races. In the new cities that sprung up on the long desecrated sites of Hindu pilgrimage—such as Mathurá and Brindaban—the temples were constructed on the same ground plan, and exhibited the same massive proportions as in the older examples that still exist at Gwalior. But the area of the interior was freed from its forest of pillars—no longer required as supports, when a vault was substituted for a roofing of stone slabs—and the walls were lightened in appearance by filling in the heads of the intercolumniations with decorative spandrels, which converted them into an arcade.

In places nearer the seat of Government, and more secular in sentiment, the predominant characteristics of the new architecture were far more distinctly Muhammadan, and the subsequent development has been entirely in that direction. What few buildings there are in Mathurá of the 16th century, are of strongly Hindu type, though built for Muhammadan uses; but even there the modification has been rapid and continuous, and the whole series of temples erected since 1803—the first year of British government and of settled peace—have domes and cupolas and arches, on the same constructural principles and with the same style of panel and moulding and surface-carving as in a mosque.

The distinctive Hindu spire, or *sikhara*, is still frequently erected, especially in country places and over shrines of Mahádev, but it is often in connection with a dome over the porch or other secondary part of the building, and its proportions have become so debased that the days of its survival are evidently numbered. From shattered fragments of most of the religious edifices of the present day—provided they bear no inscription nor betray any reference to ritual uses—it will be as difficult for an archæologist of the future to determine whether they are of Hindu or Muhammadan origin, as it is now to decide between the claims of Brahmanist and Jain to relics of mediæval India. To speak of Jain architecture, as is generally done, is altogether erroneous. What is so called is simply the style of national architecture that prevailed throughout the country, and was used indiscriminately by both classes alike, at the time when the Jains happened to be most flourishing. Thus the larger temple in the Gwalior

Fort is quoted by Mr. Fergusson as a specimen of Jain architecture and is said to be dedicated to Padma-náth, the sixth Tirthankar. A very slight amount of research has proved it to be dedicated to the Brahmanical Divinity, Vishnu, under his title of Padma-páni; whence the mistake.*

As the oldest Hindu architecture of which we have any remains shows clear traces of Greek influence, and as the longer predominance of the Muhammadan power has still more thoroughly subdued the indigenous art of mediæval India, so it must be expected that English fashions will be largely represented in the artistic development of the immediate future. The change is inevitable, and, in so far as it is a witness to historical facts, its avoidance would not be absolutely desirable, even if it were possible; for all ultra purism is unnatural, unhealthy, and bad. "When the assimilation of new matter ceases, decay must begin." Still, the amalgamation to be complete, must be gradual. Most assuredly the interests of art will not be furthered by the hasty adoption of the Italian style in its supposed entirety, but too often without much knowledge of it, except in a very debased form, as exhibited in some of the new palaces of our greatest feudatories; nor yet by adding pseudo-Gothic tracery and pinnacles to a barrack shell, as in the Agra College; but rather by an assimilation, which is suggestive of foreign culture, but translates it into Indian language, instead of literally repeating it. That this can be done by the best of our native masons, if they are allowed to work out their own ideas without too minute instructions, is, I think, sufficiently attested by the very pleasing facade of a house built last year at Khurja for Lálá Jánaki Prasád, a rich banker of that town, and a member of the Municipal Committee. The correctness of the design is impaired by the insertion of some false stone-doors on the ground floor, which are treated exactly as if made of wood.

* Mr. Fergusson speaks of this temple as 'the Sás Bahu,' which is an impossible designation. There are two temples close together on the Gwalior rock, and as one of them is a miniature of the other, natives call the two 'the Sás Bahu,' *i. e.* the mother-in-law and daughter-in-law. But neither of the two can separately bear the double name. The expression that he required to meet his meaning would be 'the larger of the Sás Bahu temples,' or simply 'the Sás.' This eminent art critic boasts of having spent ten years in India, but he does not seem to have taken the trouble to learn a single Indian language, ancient or modern. Yet a smattering of Philology would have been of considerable service to him in his archæological researches. Such a solecism as the above would then have been impossible, as also his misconception with regard to the title of the great Mártand temple in Kashmir.

In themselves they are pretty enough, but they are still an offence against propriety, since solid stone is a material of which no real door would be made. The defect is characteristic of the old native habit of thought, which was seldom much distressed by the incongruous. In other respects the design appears to me to be eminently typical of the higher Indian civilization of the nineteenth century, conservative of the national genius, but open to European refinements. The lace-like tracery of the pierced panels, the surface sculpture of others, the general grouping, no less than the details of the ornamentation, are all oriental in character; while, at the same time, the colonnade could never have been what it is, but for the influence of Italian design. The building is still unfinished and wants its parapet, which will add greatly to its beauty.

The art revival, which in the minor luxuries and conveniences of life, has of late years effected so much in England, has even there as yet made no very profound impression on architectural methods. It is still almost as true as when Ruskin framed the indictment twenty years ago, that all the pleasure, which the people of the nineteenth century take in art, is in pictures, sculpture, minor objects of virtu, or mediæval architecture, which we enjoy under the term picturesque: no pleasure is taken anywhere in modern buildings; the reason being that modern European architecture, working as it does on known rules and from given models, is not an art, but a manufacture. No true art, whether expressing itself in words, colours, or stones, says the same thing over and over again: the merit of architectural as of every other art, consists in its saying new and different things: to repeat itself is no more a characteristic of genius in brick and stone than it is of genius in verse or prose. In British India so little is this recognized, that "standard plans" are provided at head-quarters for every class of public building, and are forced upon universal acceptance throughout the length and breadth of the province, with little or no regard to local conditions as regards material, or the habits of the people, or the capacity of the workmen. Such uniformity is certainly not conducive to convenience of design, excellence of construction, or economy in expenditure; but it probably facilitates the orderly arrangement of the records in the central bureau, and is therefore highly approved by departmental authorities. As an example of the pitch to which this passion for stereotyped forms is sometimes carried, I remember noting in one large Municipality that the principal official buildings—the school, the dispensary, and the Committee-rooms—were all of exactly the same pattern, and were indistinguishable from one another, save by the inscription over the door.

It is scarcely necessary to observe that such soulless and depressing monotony is entirely the result of action from above. It is altogether uncongenial to the oriental mind, and is copied only for the same reason that induces a Marwari matron to blacken her lips and teeth, because it is better to submit to a disfigurement than to be out of the fashion : and thus we come to an adequate explanation of the mistaken idea, which so many people entertain, that architecture in India is no longer a living art. The native community, as has been already allowed, are not conscious of the artistic vitality that still animates their handicraftsmen, while many of the buildings that the latter erect are conspicuous examples of the very worst taste. But the mason who executes the work has seldom prepared the design ; or, if he has done so, he has been hampered by the necessity of subordinating his own ideas to those of his employer. In every age and in every country, the upper and moneyed classes are too materialized to have any intelligent appreciation of art. They understand the fashionable, and are ready to admire the magnificent ; but the more delicate refinements of design, which constitute the special charm of the artist's conception, and which it is the student's greatest delight to trace and interpret, are mostly lost upon them. There is no reason to suppose that the impressive attributes of St. Mark's at Venice were ever more appreciated by its ordinary votaries than at the present day, when its storied walls are unread and unheeded. The artist of old—as now—enjoyed the act of creation for its own sake ; the populace takes over the finished product, and values it more from material than from æsthetic considerations.

In India, almost the only class in the native community that still encourages indigenous art, is the much abused trader and money-lender. Not that he is moved to do so by any artistic bias, but simply by force of habit. If he decides upon building a new porch to his house, he calls in the mason of most repute in the neighbourhood, shows him the site and explains what is wanted. Perhaps the materials in whole or in part are also supplied, but the workman is then left to his own devices, on the presumption that he best understands his own business ; in the same way as a tailor, after taking his customer's measure, and being furnished with as much cloth as he wants, would be trusted to turn out a garment properly stitched, of the desired description, and of the same cut as other people wear. The result of this confidence is ordinarily most satisfactory to both parties: the workman's manual labour is relieved by the sense of independence, and is elevated by the exercise of thought; while the paymaster attends to his ordinary affairs during the progress of the undertaking, and in the end gets his money's worth as in any ordinary mercantile transaction. But having once dismissed the builder—as if to prove how little he cares for art in the abstract—the owner generally proceeds to disfigure his new possession by blocking up a niche or two with mud or clumsy masonry, screening the arch with a piece of tattered matting, or smearing the jambs of the doorway with daubs of red paint and whitewash.

The gain to artistic interests, and the saving to the Exchequer, would be enormous, if a similar amount of reasonable confidence in its employés were exhibited by Government in the execution of its public works. It need not really regard æsthetic considerations any more highly than the typical *baniya* does; but it would get its work done well and cheaply, and thus would not forfeit its character for practical common sense, even though some traces of good design still survived after many years of utilitarian ill-usage.

A happy example of thoroughly Hindu treatment, as practised at the present day in the absence of any direction from without, is afforded by a small, but very elaborate, gateway, for which the town of Khurja is indebted to Lála Lachhman Dás, a well-to-do trader, who is remodelling his house in the bazar there; the work being designed and carried out by Dhúla, a Bráhman architect, who lives at the neighbouring town of Háthras, in the Aligarh district. A photograph would be impossible; for though the main façade of the house looks on to a fairly broad street, the porch stands in a little side lane which is scarcely broad enough for two foot passengers to walk abreast. The introduction of animal sculpture, the exuberance of surface decoration, and the unsuitableness of the site selected for its display, are all features curiously characteristic of the best and worst points in the Hindu craftsman. In his devotion to the perfect rendering of each separate detail, as it comes under his hand, he too little considers the ultimate destination of the whole; while any faculty for reproducing the beauty of the human or other animate form has been completely destroyed by ages of desuetude. He is thus content to repeat the archaic rudeness of his temple-gods, in which the discouragement of Muhammadan rule has so long forbidden improvement, that the eye has at last learnt to acquiesce in their familiar uncouthness.

If the mercantile classes of native society are distinguished by their conservative adherence to ancestral usage, the landed gentry, who are on visiting terms with European officials, cherish equally strong aspirations in the opposite direction. To relieve the monotony of their eventless life, many of them spend large sums of money every year in building, and keep a native architect as a regular member of their domestic establishment. But he is warned that nothing in Hindustani style can be tolerated ; some Government office, in the civil station, or the last new barracks in the nearest military cantonments, are the palatial edifices which he is expected to emulate. To give an example : On the top of the Bulandshahr hill is a school, erected twenty years ago, with a small bell-turret which apears to have been designed by the engineer of the period as an exact copy of the Bethesda, or Little Zoar, that forms such a familiar sight in the back lanes of an English manufacturing town. The idea has been so successfully accomplished, that every European visitor at once concludes it to be a methodist place of worship, and enquires to what particular denomination it belongs. The style of architecture may be readily imagined without further illustration. But, as it is a Government building, it sets the fashion, and, not long ago, the native gentleman of highest rank in the district, intimated to me that he wished to add a clock-tower to his country house, and that he proposed to make it a *fac simile* of this delightful structure at Bulandshahr.

This little incident shows how important it is that the public taste should be correctly guided, not only by direct educational institutions, such as schools of art, museums and exhibitions, but still more by the persistent stimulus of practical example. So long as the necessity for the latter is ignored, the former tend rather to the isolation of the artist and the restriction of art influences to the connoisseur, instead of bringing them to bear upon society at large. In the words of the resolution, which prefaces the Indian Art Journal, "there can be no reasonable doubt that the upper classes of the native community would gladly follow the example of the Government, and cherish all that is best in indigenous art ;" but in architec-

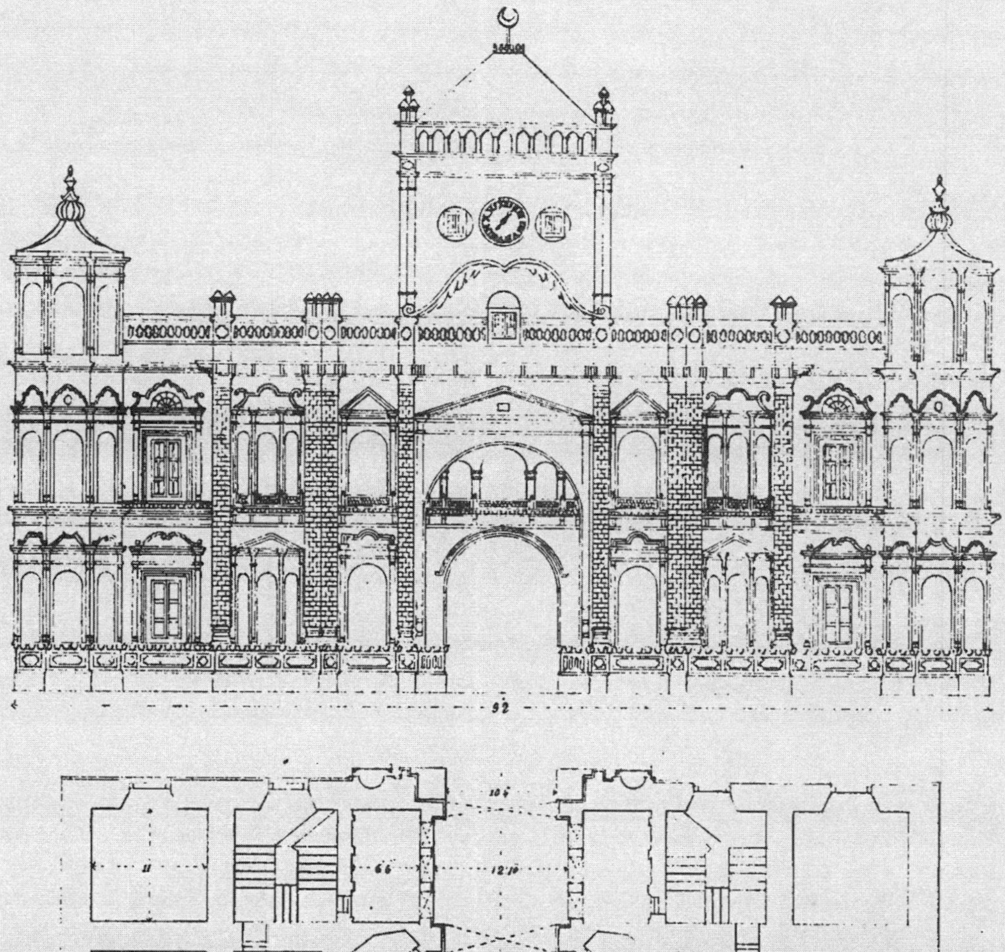

ARCHITECTURE AS UNDERSTOOD BY THE NATIVE GENTRY.

DÁNPUR GATE.

ture, at all events, which is the mother of all the arts, the example unfortunately has as yet been never given.

A partial explanation of the neglect may perhaps be found in the fact that, so far as the Supreme Government is concerned, circumstances have allowed it no option. It has been obliged to import foreign models; for neither in the swamps of Calcutta, nor on the heights of Simla, has any indigenous form of architecture been available for adoption. The Bengali has simply a talent for imitation, and has never invented a style for himself in any branch of art; while the Himalayan mountaineer was too backward in civilization to feel any need for it. With most of the Provincial Governments the case is far different. They are seated in the centres of old Indian culture. But the fashion of occidentalism, however incongruous with the local environment, has permeated from above; and the only patronage hitherto vouchsafed to native architecture is limited to an artificial and purely scholastic form, in the restoration of the dead past, and is not extended to the development of the living present.

A shocking travesty of Italian, or rather French design, is exhibited in a gateway, which one of the principal Muhammadan gentlemen in the district has had under construction for the last three or four years. It forms the entrance to the courtyard of his family residence at Dánpur, and is of considerable dimensions, being 92 feet long and 70 feet deep. The cost will be in proportion, and it is truly lamentable that want of taste and the influence of bad example should be thus conspicuously illustrated. The incongruous quasi-Indian plinth, in conjunction with an attenuated order of tall rusticated pilasters supporting imitation chimneypots, and the clumsy carpentry of the windows with their jerky and most ungainly dressing and ill-proportioned pediments, make up a *tout ensemble*, which for rococo vulgarity, could scarcely be surpassed. The material is stone, but it requires a close inspection to realize the fact; the extreme coarseness of all the details being so much more suggestive of plaster. In spite of ridicule and remonstrance, and repeated offers to supply a design more in harmony with national precedent, my friend has an unanswerable rejoinder:—" The works, he says, which are carried out under your direction, however pleasing in themselves, have the one fatal drawback that they are not stamped with official approval. In fact, one of them was denounced by a competent departmental authority as an absolute 'eye-sore.' Nothing in the same style is ever undertaken by Government. Your buildings fitly express your own peculiarity of temperament, but the personal predilection for Indian forms is only a weakness or eccentricity; such designs would be out of harmony with my own more advanced views, which are all in favour of English fashions. The trading classes do well to adhere to Hindustani types, but the landed gentry prefer to range themselves with their rulers, and thus to emphasize their distinction from the vulgar." When I further object that his façade is incorrect even from the European point of view he cannot understand how that is possible. In the same way as Christianity is popularly identified with any denial of religious obligation, so the essence of European architecture is supposed to consist in a reckless disregard of all recognized canons of ornament and proportion. Any outcast is dubbed a Christian, and any ugliness in a building is accounted European. Now that I have had a special drawing made of his gate, he will be more than ever convinced that my criticisms were simply prompted by deficient intelligence, and that he has at last taught me to admire what I once ignorantly disparaged.

A gateway, in a very different style, has lately been added to his house at Bulandshahr by Maulvi Muhammad Bakhsh, the Honorary Magistrate of Chaprávat. It is of special interest as showing the readiness with which the upper classes would return to the true principles of indigenous architecture, if only it were more generally in fashion. The gate is in two stories, with a deeply recessed single arch below; the plinth, shafts and spandrels of which are covered with most delicate diapers and foliage. The balcony above has slender piers of pierced tracery, and its three arches have their heads filled in with stone fan-lights, below which they are fitted with doors of common-place English pattern. These are the solitary defect in the design, and fortunately it is one which admits of an easy remedy. The combination of depth and solidity in the mass with lightness of touch in the ornamental details indicates a true artistic faculty of conception, and the idea has been carried out with much technical skill.

Our engineers' buildings, as a rule, have the one merit of simplicity. They make no pretence of pleasing the eye, but neither do they often wilfully offend it by an obtrusive display of misplaced architectural embellishment. Considered as temporary makeshifts for the deposit of departmental returns, or the casual shelter of distressed officials, they might pass uncriti-

CHAPRÁVAT GATE, BULANDSHAHR. 1882.

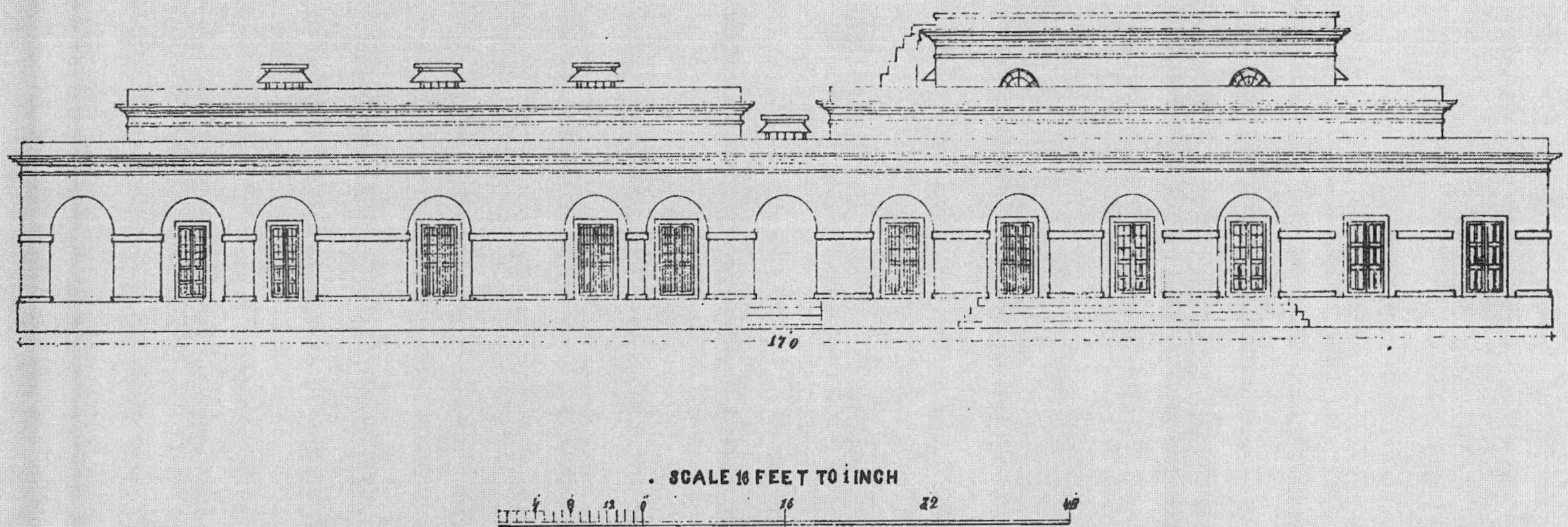

ARCHITECTURE AS UNDERSTOOD BY THE PUBLIC WORKS DEPARTMENT

THE DISTRICT LAW COURTS.

cized. But, unfortunately, the people of the country will not regard them from this purely utilitarian point of view. The Government is omnipotent, and if it chooses to lodge its servants at equal cost in sheds and godowns instead of in courts and palaces, it must be not from want of thought or skill, but because it deliberately prefers the shed and godown style of construction. The latter is, therefore, the style which loyal subjects are bound to adopt, if they would be in harmony with their rulers.

The most important Government building in the Bulandshahr district is the set of Law Courts and Revenue Offices at head-quarters. The façade, which is 170 feet in length, may be adequately described as a long low wall pierced with a uniform row of round-headed cavities. There is no porch, nor any other feature by which to distinguish the front from the back, nor on either side is any one doorway marked off from its fellows as a main entrance. The design would answer equally well, or indeed much better for a dry goods store, a barrack, or a factory. No stranger, unfamiliar with the economic eccentricities of Anglo-Indian administration, could for a moment suppose that a building of such a mean and poverty-stricken appearance represented the dignity of the Empire to about a million of people, and was the fiscal centre of a district contributing over fourteen lacs of rupees to the annual revenue of the State. It might, perhaps, be imagined that external dignity had been judiciously disregarded in order to secure a maximum of internal convenience ; but if such was the intention, it has signally failed of attainment ; the paltry appearance of the exterior only prepares the eye for the still greater shabbiness of everything inside.

The buildings, to which the remainder of this article will be devoted, have been designed and carried out in the hope of stemming the tide of utilitarian barbarism, which had swamped Bulandshahr as completely as every other part of the Province. In April 1878, when I took over charge of the district, the only two buildings in it, ancient or modern, of the slightest architectural pretension, were a ruinous tomb of Sháhjahan's reign at Kásna, and an unfinished stone pavilion of somewhat later date at Shikárpur. The four Municipalities had each been provided, about twenty years previously, by the energy of the then Collector, with a complete set of public institutions—school, dispensary, and post-office—all substantially constructed of good brick and mortar, but on regulation patterns of the severest type, without any concession to local sentiment. The principal citizens, in their shops and dwelling-houses, had followed the example thus set, and were everywhere repeating the same dreariness of design, only in inferior materials and with less careful execution. It is too often forgotten by those in authority that it is only the perfection of its mechanical finish which, in European work, often compensates in part for the want of artistic originality. By combining the poverty of western invention with the clumsiness of eastern technique, the characteristic virtues of both races are sacrificed. Yet, this is the plan which is systematically adopted throughout British India. The design for a new church or town-hall is supplied by an English engineer, who openly avows his ignorance of architecture; while the execution is left to native workmen. The latter inherit the artistic traditions of the country, but are unskilled in the management of modern mechanical appliances, and are utterly untaught in the principles of European style, so that they cannot appreciate either the boldness of a Gothic moulding, or the elegance of contour and proportion upon which mainly depends the charm of a Grecian order.

It was not thus that the Muhammadans, the earlier conquerors of India, achieved those architectural triumphs in mosque and palace, which we now conscientiously restore with many expressions of idle admiration, but apparently without gathering much practical instruction from the method they inculcate. Their accurate reproduction is undoubtedly in itself an excellent undertaking and one that reflects the highest credit on the Government, but the functions of design are not vitally stimulated, nor is art adequately encouraged by an exclusive devotion to the past. The general outline of any large scheme of improvement, and the site and ground plan of the different buildings that are to be grouped together, are matters upon which the Hindu—with his overpowering passion for detail—does well to follow foreign guidance. The execution also will be largely benefited in evenness by European supervision; but the composition of the façade and all the details of the decoration are best left to the craftsmen who will have to execute them. In working out their own conceptions, or repeating the familiar types of local tradition, both mind and hand will act more freely than when they are set to copy forms and mouldings, which they have never practised and do not understand. The carpenters and bricklayers whom I have employed at Bulandshahr are, for the most part, the very same men who raised the bare walls, and set up the tasteless door frames that distinguish the older public buildings of the town. Nor do they ask any higher pay for the more decorative work upon which they are now engaged. If the present results are more attractive to the eye, the improvement is solely due to an improved method of direction on the lines above indicated. It is a sound maxim of administration, which holds good in small matters as in large, that it is well to trust the people you employ; if you cannot trust a man, do not employ him. An Englishman's function in India is to stimulate enterprize and direct the general course of affairs, but to abstain from interference with the details of execution. No character more lowers the prestige of Government than "the zealous official," who trusts no one but himself even in the pettiest details, for which subordinates are entertained, and who thus loses the broad view which he alone is in a position to command, and which, if he loses it, is lost altogether.

The architectural designs of the new buildings at Bulandshahr do not profess to exhibit any novel features of very remarkable artistic merit. On the contrary, whatever value attaches to them, is to be found in their easy and unconscious adherence to ordinary traditional practice, and in the consequent absence of any exceptionally striking effects. There has been no intentional imitation of older buildings, but, at the same time, there has been no straining after originality. The towers and gateways and arcades of modern Bulandshahr claim to be congruous and picturesque, but only in the same way as the streets of a mediæval English town, which could be matched by others of similar character all over the country. Then—as still in India—the influence of the prevalent style was not so much inculcated in the studio as felt in the air. With some few local modifications, in matters of detail, arising chiefly from the ingenious utilization of local materials, such as the cut-flint panelling in Norfolk and Suffolk, and the Purbeck marble shafts of the western counties, the *motif* of Gothic work at any given period was similar in essentials from the Tweed to the Land's End. Between the sculptured decoration of a Cathedral and that in a village church there may often be a superiority of finish in the former, the result of the more extensive practice acquired by working in the midst of a large community; but this advantage of facile manipulation, with its tendency to stereotype invention, was often outweighed by the greater leisure and unconventionality of the rural artisan. Unless new inspiration and invention come to guide it, the predominance of technical skill in art invariably ends in degradation of the artist's function. Man was not intended to work with the accuracy of a machine; and, in architecture, slight irregularities, which an engineer would condemn as unpardonable defects, are on the contrary the inseparable accidents of individual effort, and as evidences of its exercise, please rather than offend the educated eye. Human faculties will never succeed in realizing their ideal; but still it is a nobler part to form an ideal and struggle towards it, than to rest content with the easy attainment of stereotyped mediocrity. If the system that I advocate, *viz.*, the free employment of local talent, unhampered by departmental interference, were adopted throughout India, there might be occasional failures, but it is reasonable to expect there would also be brilliant successes; and the failures must be numerous indeed before they produced at all the same depressing effect as the present deadness of uniformity.

Of all the new improvements in the town, the first that I undertook was the construction of a terrace, which once a week is used for a market. The site was an untidy road-side strip on the top of the hill, immediately opposite the Tahsili Gate. It has been converted into a paved platform in two stages, 194 feet long and 28 feet broad, made of brick, with a cut-stone edging. An arcade at the back, which forms a convenient place of deposit for bales of cloth and other perishable goods in case of a storm, is also mainly of brick construction, and is a pleasing specimen of local skill. But so much time and labour were involved in cutting each separate brick into shape for the slender rounded and fluted shafts, that the ultimate expense was scarcely, if at all, less than if stone had been employed. I have therefore never repeated the experiment on a similar scale, and have restricted the application of ornamental brick work to small niches and similar details, where it has an excellent effect. The cost of the work was Rs. 1,600, the whole of which has been already recovered by the annual income from the market-dues. The money for this improvement was obtained by the sale of a small plot of confiscated ground close by, which had belonged to the rebel Abdul Latif. The purchaser, Kunvar Maháráj Sinh, intended to build a house upon it, which would have been an additional improvement; but he died before the walls were more than a few feet above the ground.

The next enterprise was the Bathing Ghat on the river bank. The foundation stone was laid on the 1st November 1878, but the completion of the work was delayed for two years by the officiousness of an Executive

MARKET TERRACE, BULANDSHAHR. 1879.

Engineer who represented to Government that it would spoil the look of the adjoining bridge, and would be nothing short of "an eye-sore." Fortunately the work was eventually allowed to proceed, and the effect of both buildings, though they are in very different styles of architecture, is greatly enhanced by the juxtaposition. Ordinary intelligence might have foreseen this result; and that such obstructive counsels should have been suffered to prevail so long against local enterprise, is a typical illustration of the difficulties that beset a district officer. He is placed in a position which apparently commands almost unlimited capabilities for doing good; but he soon discovers that, in whatever direction he attempts to move, some head of a department is already on the spot, watching to trip him up. As the river forms the boundary of the town to the east, and all the roads from that direction converge at the bridge, the ghát, with its four graceful towers, is seen from a considerable distance by travellers as they approach their destination. The total cost was Rs. 16,373. Of this sum Rs. 3,670 were contributed by the Municipality; the remainder had been raised by public subscription. As in all river-works, the most difficult and the most expensive part of the undertaking was the sinking of the wells for the foundation. This was all successfully accomplished without any professional assistance. The towers are octagonal in shape, of solid brick masonry, faced with slabs of red sandstone cut into panels and set in white stone frames. On two of these panels are recorded the names of all the subscribers, arranged in order according to the amount of their donations. These towers are finished off at the top with brackets and eaves, above which is a plinth supporting an open kiosque with a domed roof, the pinnacle of which rises to a height of 52 feet from the ground. The kiosques of the two towers that spring from the base of the steps are approached from the upper terrace on the road-side, and form pleasant places in which to sit and look out upon the river. The other two kiosques on the water's edge are unfortunately inaccessible, as the open screen-walls intended to connect them with the pair behind were vetoed on the ground that they might obstruct the stream. The stone pavement between the four towers has now become a favourite stage for the theatrical performances that are generally held during the festival of the *Holi*, when a canopy is stretched over the area, and the spectators throng the steps. Here too, a display of fireworks takes place during the week of the Annual District Show, some of them being let off at the foot of the steps, and others from the opposite bank, whence they are reflected in the stream. With the arches and parapet of the bridge marked out with lines of tiny lamps and the elegant architecture of the kiosques illuminated by hanging globes and chandeliers, the restless crowd as it breaks up into ever-changing groups and bright-coloured masses amidst the tinselled torch stands and flaring flambeaux, produces a series of kaleidoscopic effects before the eyes of the European spectators, who witness it from their seats at the top of the steps, which could only be imitated in England on the stage of a London theatre.

In addition to the main ghát, the opposite side of the stream is also provided with a short flight of stone steps, of equally substantial construction; and above the bridge are a Go-ghát, or slope for watering cattle, and two arcaded rest-houses, of good and ornamental brick masonry, which are generally crowded with poor travellers, who are allowed to stay there for 24 hours. These two buildings cost a further sum of Rs. 944, about half of which was a wedding gift from a Thakur, who preferred to spend the money in this way, rather than waste it in feeding a horde of lazy Brahmans, as is the custom on such occasions. No where else in the whole length of its winding course can the little river boast of possessing so handsome and complete a set of artistic adornments.

In imitation of the precedent thus established, the Hindu residents of the town are now building a second Ghát, a little higher up the stream, in connection with the temple of Rámesvar. This they propose to call 'the Lachhman Ghát,' in honour of Rája Lachhman Sinh, who has been a Deputy Collector in the district for the long period of 17 years, and who is highly and deservedly esteemed by all classes of the community. He is not only one of the most able Revenue officers in the service, but he is also a man of scholarly tastes and literary acquirements: two of his vernacular translations from the Sanskrit—the Sakuntalá in prose and the Megha-dúta in verse are excellent specimens of pure and elegant Hindi composition. He has also compiled in English a Memoir of the district, which is full of accurate information on all matters of local interest.

From the town side the bridge and ghát are approached by a spacious thoroughfare, 150 feet wide, with a double row of trees, where a market is held twice a week, which is largely attended by the people of the neighbouring villages, for dealings in cloth and miscellaneous petty wares

BATHING GHÁT, BULANDSHAHR 1880.

and agricultural produce. This road is all of made earth, raised eight feet above the level of the low river meadows, and is bordered north and south by lines of shops, which, with their verandahs, are 32 feet deep. Thus the road with its shops forms a solid stone-faced embankment 214 feet wide, and is 700 feet in length.

At the back of the shops, on the north side towards the open country, is a walled enclosure, comprising an area of nearly four acres, used as a paráo, or camping-ground for vehicles of all descriptions; and on the south side is a Saráe, or hostel for travellers. The shops, as seen from the central road-way, are only one story high; but from the low ground at the back they show a basement story besides, with vaulted cells, which are used as stables on the paráo side, and as travellers' quarters on the other. The entire cost of this extensive project up to the present time has been Rs. 56,416, including Rs. 9,800 for the actual embankment, Rs. 2,000 for the paráo wall and Rs. 900 for a masonry verandah to the Saráe rooms. The balance, *viz.*, Rs. 43,716, was the cost of the shops.

Immediately opposite the ghát, the basement floor of the embankment is widened out into a spacious crypt-like building of five aisles, 70 feet long, which has direct access to the river by a subterranean passage carried under the roadway. This was constructed at a cost of Rs. 4,833, which was mainly defrayed by Chaudhri Lachhman Sinh of Sikárpur, an Honorary Magistrate, and one of the wealthiest landed proprietors in the district, who made the donation as a thankoffering after recovery from a very severe illness. It is used as a Dharmsála, or rest-house for the poor, and is admirably adapted for the purpose from its coolness and its situation at the very entrance of the town, in close proximity both to the river and the market.

The shops on the embankment are divided into four blocks, of which three, containing in all 46 shops, have been completed; the fourth is postponed till such time as the increasing trade of the town may require it. Each line is broken in the centre by a gateway, one leading into the paráo, the other on to a new street, which communicates with the saráe and the main bazar of the town. The depth of both these gates allows of the construction of an upper room with the fair interior dimensions of 18 feet by 20. One room is on the point of completion, and will serve for the ordinary monthly meetings of the Municipal Committee, who have hitherto had no place of their own in which to assemble. It has a projecting stone balcony at each end, and the windows are filled with stone tracery. The cost thus far has been Rs. 4,000. The room over the opposite gate will be taken in hand next year.

The embankment was not quite finished on the 19th September 1880, when the heavy rain occurred which caused the fatal landslip at Naini Tál. The river rose suddenly from 13 to nearly 21 feet in height, the greatest recorded height for any previous flood being 16½ feet, and in order to save the bridge a breach was made in the road on the other side of the stream. This was rapidly widened by the force of the torrent into a chasm three furlongs broad. But for the embankment, the roadway to the west of the bridge must also have gone, and the greater part of the town would then have been destroyed. Even as it was, much damage was caused by the back-water which spread up into the streets from the lower bend of the river ; exposure to the direct forces of the current would have had much more serious results. An insignificant rivulet made its way over the embankment through the spaces left for the gateways ; but the masonry walls—though the mortar was scarcely dry—stood the shock well, and fully justified the cost of their construction even from a purely utilitarian point of view. It may also be mentioned that the shops let some for Rs. 4 and some for Rs. 5 a month each, which gives a return of over 6 per cent. on the outlay.

On emerging from the low land, the embankment is continued towards the west, first at the same width of 150 feet through a bazar, in which the frontage of the shops has been remodelled by the proprietor Munshi Gopál Ráe,* so as to assimilate it in appearance with the Municipal work, and then as an ordinary street till it reaches the Collector's house and grounds, which are the beginning of the European quarter. At this

---

* Munshi Gopál Ráe is a native of the town, where he has a fine house and owns a large amount of property, but being in Government service—he is now a Deputy Collector in the Gonda district—he is seldom resident. He is perhaps the only person who has been a sufferer by the recent improvements. Before the shops on the embankment were built, his were always let at a high rent—though they were very wretched places—Now most of them are unoccupied, though the rent has been greatly reduced and they have been put in much better order than ever before. However, he bears his loss with singular good-temper, and seems honestly to consider himself compensated by the improved appearance of the town, where he hopes to spend his old age and where his family has been settled for many generations.

point of junction, a large masonry reservoir, called the Lyall Tank, has now been constructed by public subscription at a cost of Rs. 16,000. The first stone was laid by the Lieutenant-Governor of the Province, Sir Alfred Lyall, on the 7th February 1883, when he re-visited Bulandshahr for the first time after an interval of 26 years since the Mutiny, when he was attached to the district as a junior civilian, and greatly distinguished himself in the military operations against the rebels. The aqueduct, by which water will be obtained from a distributary of the Ganges Canal, about a mile distant, has not yet been commenced, but an allotment of Rs. 2,500 has been made for it in the Municipal Budget, and the tank itself is finished. It measures 230 feet square and is 14 feet deep. The whole of the earth procured by the excavation has been utilized in raising the level of the streets and open places in the town, thereby greatly improving its drainage and sanitation. Tiers of steps and platforms reach from the top to the floor of the tank, and on each side are broken up into three compartments by dwarf towers, based on the lowest platform and rising to the level of the outer margin, with which they are connected by screen walls. The top of these is broadened out by stone slabs over a bold cornice, so as to form footpaths for reaching the roof of the towers, which makes either a pleasant seat or a convenient projection for bathers to dive from. The central compartment, on the east side, has no steps, but is cut back into a long paved slope with flanking walls for watering cattle.

West of the tank is the Moti Bagh, an area of eleven acres, lately levelled and enclosed at a cost of Rs. 6,150, and now in process of conversion into a public garden. Part of it was formerly a broad and deep ravine, which brought down into the town the drainage of all the surrounding country and passed it out into the river through the arch which has been already mentioned, as now making the river gate of Chaudhri Lachhman Siṅh's Dharmsála. On the edge of this ravine was an extensive mound, known as the Moti Bazár, which, many hundreds of years ago, had been an inhabited site. In levelling it to fill up the ravine, besides other minor curiosities, a clay seal was found inscribed with the owner's name, apparently of the fifth century A. D., together with an immense number of large bricks, a cubit long, and half a cubit broad, and many curious specimens of a local terracotta manufactory. These objects are mostly of a cocoanut shape, and seem to have been intended either for vases or for architectural finials. A fine statue of Buddha, of the 8th century, had been previously discovered on the same spot.

In this new garden, close by the roadside, from which it is divided only by a low wall with stone posts and chains, is now being built the Town Hall, which, if I am able to superintend its completion, will be one of the most remarkable modern buildings in the Province. The cost will scarcely be less than Rs. 30,000, the whole of which is being defrayed by the munificence of a single individual, Rájá Bákir Ali Khán, of Pindrával. He received the decoration of a C. I. E. from the hands of the Lieutenant-Governor in the building itself on the 7th February 1883, when a temporary roof was thrown over the unfinished walls for the occasion. The hall, the lower end of which can be screened off as an ante-room, measures 80 feet by 25, and will be about 30 feet high, with a range of clerestory windows under the cornice. It is intended that in design, construction, and all its accessories it should form a complete epitome of all the indigenous arts and industries of the neighbourhood. The roof of the verandah is an elaborate piece of carpentry, and two pairs of doors, as specimens of wood-carving and inlaying, were contributed on loan to the Calcutta Exhibition, where they attracted much attention, and were awarded a certificate of the first-class and a gold medal. A copy of another pair of its doors was made by request, and is now deposited in the South Kensington Museum. The stone work of the porch and verandah and of the great arches of the hall is of equally conspicuous merit, and a little wicket gate in the low roadside wall, immediately in front of the north verandah, is supported by ramps which are scarcely to be surpassed as graceful specimens of stone foliage.

In addition to this minor entrance in direct connection with the Town Hall, the Moti Bagh is provided with two great gates. The one in the east wall, immediately opposite the Lyall Tank, is being erected in memory of Mr. Elliot Colvin, the late Commissioner of the Division, whose sudden and untimely death, on the 3rd November 1883, was deeply felt by all classes of the community. It is estimated to cost about Rs. 4,000, and should be completed by the end of this year. The main gate is on the opposite side, towards the west, and will perpetuate the name of Ráo Umráo Sinh of Kachesar, who has given Rs. 4,500 for its construction. Its archway, which towards the road is of white sand-stone, covered with delicate surface tracery, is flanked by two rooms of block-kankar masonry, with red-brick turrets at the corners, surmounted by domed and pinnacled stone kiosques 46 feet high. The rooms are intended as lodges for the gardener and watchman, and have an upper unroofed story with arcaded fronts of red brick, the whole being surmounted by a parapet of white stone posts and panels. The variety of colour afforded by the employment of so many different materials and styles of construction affords a pleasing effect, and is to some extent a novelty. There was formerly a superstitious prejudice in the native mind against the use of block kankar except for under-ground work, such as wells and foundations; and a trader, who built four of the shops on the embankment on his own responsibility, refused to conform in this respect to the specification with which I had supplied him, and in the back-wall, where lime-stone had been used for the other shops, he substituted brick. This was afterwards plastered and pointed so as to make it look, as much as possible, like the rest of the line, but the difference cannot be concealed, and it remains a disfigurement, though being at the back it is not greatly noticed. Since then I have used it so freely and with such obvious success, that the prejudice against it may be considered as almost extinct.

Another building, which occupies a corner in the Moti Bagh, is the Station Bath. Even this peculiarly English institution has furnished an opportunity for an ingenious adaptation of oriental architecture. The tank itself is open to the sky, but is surrounded by a corridor—made double at one end for a dressing-room—with brick arcades facing the water, and solid external walls of block kankar masonry. A flight of stairs leads to the roof which is flat, and can therefore be used for taking headers from, or as a terrace commanding a pleasant view of the garden. The windows have arched wooden frames with balustrades and shutters, all elegantly carved in a variety of patterns, and the doors are a still more elaborate piece of carpentry, like those in the Town Hall. Over the entrance is a stone niche with inscriptions in English and Hindustani, recording that this gift for the use of the European residents of the station was made by Saiyid Hasan Shah, the Honorary Magistrate for the town and the vice-President of the Municipality. The cost has amounted to Rs. 3,600. The site is most convenient as the Library and Racket Court are immediately opposite. These were built some years ago and are more useful than ornamental; but they have been brought into harmony with their new surroundings, by the insertion of stone traceried windows and a pair of handsomely carved doors. Even the Race Stand, outside the station, has been built on similar principles, and is thoroughly Indian in character. The material is block kankar with dressings of white sand-stone. The cost has been gradually defrayed by the annual sale of tickets at the time of the races.

The handsomest private house in the town was built for Saiyid Mihrbán Ali, the Honorary Magistrate of Gulaothi. It occupies a singularly favorable position at the east end of a broad street, which in front of the house first opens out into a small square, and then branches off into two bazars, running due north and south. Immediately at the back is the steep slope of the hill, on which the old Fort once stood, and the rise is so rapid, that the carriage-entrance, which is up a side lane, and the court-yard on to which it opens, are on a level with the roof of the shops, which from the Square appear as a basement story to the building, and thus give a great increase of dignity to the façade. It was under construction throughout the year 1880, and the house warming took place on the 26th of the following February, on the last day of the annual Show, when all the European residents and visitors sat down to dinner with their host in the large room on the first floor. A third story with a beautiful screen of pierced stone tracery was afterwards added, making the cost of the frontage amount to Rs. 4,200. The premises at the back are extensive and commodious, but of ordinary brick masonry, and are not yet fully completed.

The central area of the Square was formerly a dusty untidy waste, but now appears as a raised brick terrace with stone dressings, and carved stone lamp-posts at the four corners. It was constructed in 1879 at a cost of about Rs. 1,000. The people were at first opposed to the improvement, thinking it might interfere with the celebration of the Bharat Miláp, the meeting of Ráma, Lakshman and Síta on their return from exile with their brother Bharat, which forms the last scene in the popular miracle play of the Rám Líla acted throughout India during the festival of the Dasahara, and which at Bulandshahr is invariably performed in this particular Square. When I witnessed it in the first year of my incumbency, all the surroundings were of the poorest and most squalid appearance; now, on all four sides, brick and carved stone have been substituted for mud and thatch, and a more effective stage for an illumination or theatrical

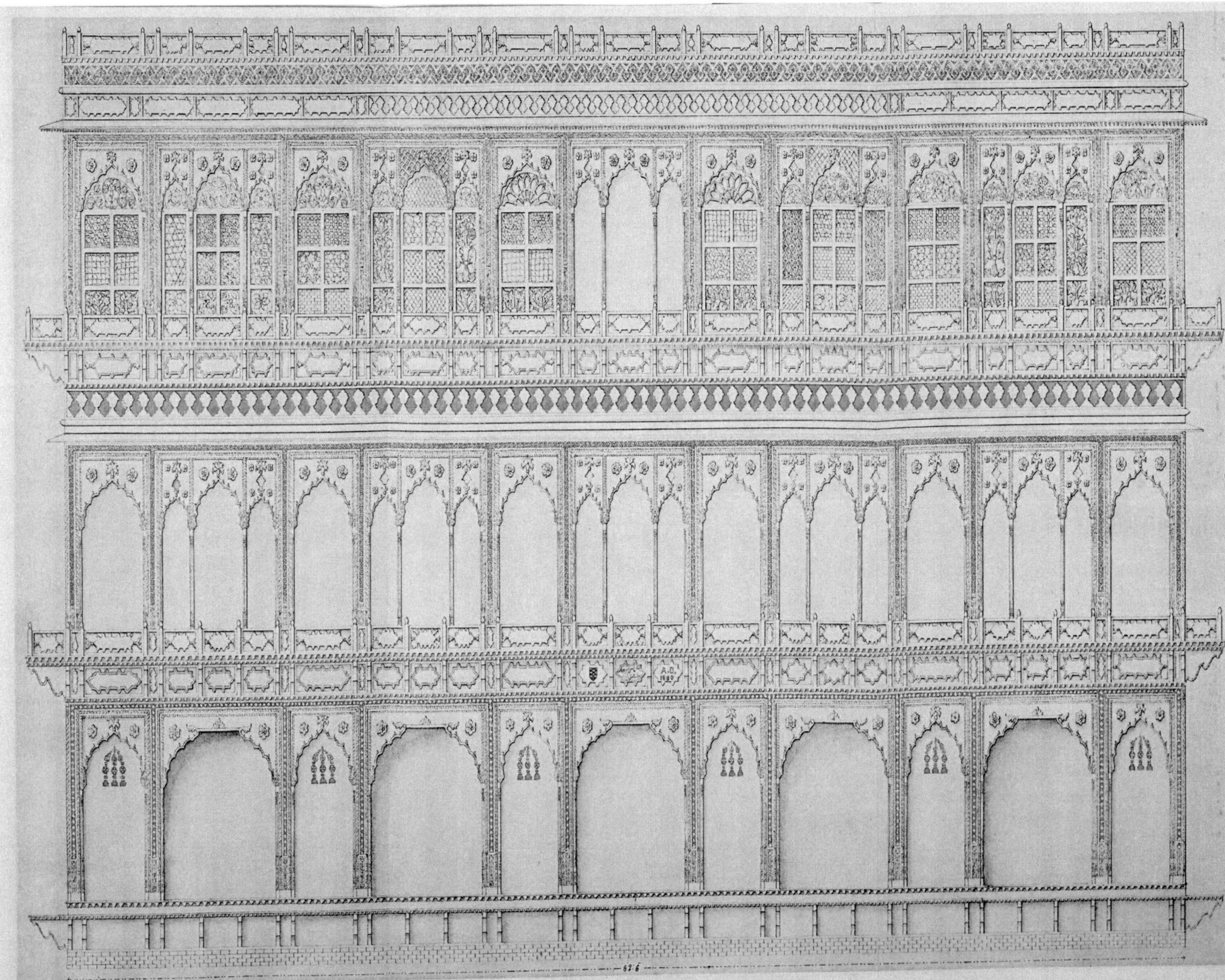

GULAOTHI HOUSE
BULANDSHAHR

performance could scarcely be found in the largest town in the Province. The successful transformation of the spot is so fully appreciated by the citizens, that since then they have readily fallen in with any scheme that I have proposed, in perfect confidence that the result will prove satisfactory. The well in the square, which is a very favourite one, with people drawing water from it all day long, at the same time that the pavement was made was cleaned and repaired and enclosed with a very elegant stone-screen at an outlay of Rs. 200. There was also added for the accommodation of a Brahman, who supplies a draught of drinking water to the thirsty wayfarer, a prettily decorated square stone cell, or *Piyáo.* This is surmounted by a lofty hexagonal shaft of masonry tapering up to a stone finial, with tier upon tier of little niches on all its sides from top to bottom, in which lamps are placed whenever there is an illumination of the town. This was the gift of Chaudhri Bijay Sinh of Sikri, and cost Rs. 500.

In a line with Mihrbán Ali's house is a temple with a high spire in the background, built by a Hindu widow. The front was first of brick, but in order not to be outdone in magnificence by her Muhammadan neighbour, it was no sooner finished than she pulled it down and re-built it in stone as it now appears.

On the north side of the square was a narrow strip of ground occupied by some miserable hovels, which I have pulled down, and in their place erected a handsome double-storied range of buildings, with seven shops in the basement, and a convenient set of rooms above which are let out as a Banker's offices. This façade also is of carved stone, with a slight intermixture of red brick. The property belongs to Munawar Ali Khan, who has the misfortune to be of weak intellect. His estate, which is a considerable one, lying chiefly in the Muradabad district, is therefore administered by the Court of Wards. The family, originally Hindu, has been connected with the town of Bulandshahr, ever since its very first settlement under the name of Baran, more than three thousand years ago. It was therefore only fitting that the scion of so ancient a stock should be locally represented by something more sightly and substantial than a ruinous line of mud hovels. Accordingly I drew attention to the matter in the proper official quarter, and eventually obtained sanction for the removal of the old tumble-down sheds—which were a disgrace to the administration of the estate—and for the expenditure of Rs. 9,000 on the new block, which was completed in 1882.

The rental at present gives a return of only 4 per cent, on the outlay ; the town so far as shops are concerned having now become a little over-built : for any sort of dwelling house there is a great demand; but the site was too contracted to be suitable for that purpose. The building, from most points of view, seems to be backed by the steep range of the castle hill, with the Tahsili on its top. This is a sombre jail-like pile, erected in 1866, at a cost of Rs, 14,187, on the site of the old Fort, the last relics of which were then demolished, and have ever since been regretted, as affording more comfortable quarters for the staff of revenue officials than their modern substitute.

A little outside the Square, on the north side of the broad street, by which, as has been already mentioned, it is approached from the west, stands another conspicuously handsome private building. This is the town residence of Muhammad Ali Khan, the Honorary Magistrate of Jahángirabád. Here also—as in Mihrbán Ali's house—the carriage entrance is from a back lane, where the ground is on a level with the roof of the shops that form the basement story of the front. A spacious stone verandah overlooks the street, and runs the whole length of the principal reception hall, which was first used on the 25th February 1882 for a dinner that wound up the festivities of the Annual Show. A stone model of the façade was ordered by Mr. Purdon Clarke as a characteristic specimen of modern Indian architecture, and has been deposited in the South Kensington Museum. The chief peculiarity of the style, which is the same as that employed in the two companion buildings already described, consists in the great depth of the apparently slender shafts that support the arcade. They cover the entire thickness of the wall on which they stand, and are thus very substantial supports, though their front shows a breadth of only two or three inches. The back ground of the frieze and string courses, and the outlines of the panels in the balcony screens, are coloured with different tints which give prominence to the carving and a general air of brightness to the whole composition. This practice is comparatively a novelty, but has at once found imitators, and is now generally adopted in all new buildings in the neighbourhood.

At the west end of this street, on opposite sides of a small open place, stand the English School and the Dispensary, both substantial buildings, erected the one in 1864, the other in 1867, under the supervision of Mr. Webster, the then Collector. The materials and construction, for

JAHANGIRABAD HOUSE
BULANDSHAHR
1881

which alone he is responsible, are of the very best description, and do him the highest credit as a practical builder.

The designs were supplied by Government engineers, and have the usual departmental defects of low plinth, inadequate cornice, and the absence of any staircase on to the roof. The Assistant Surgeon's dwelling-house close by is a typical specimen of professional wrong headedness. It is absolutely uninhabitable, being sunk in a sort of well which prevents the possibility either of drainage or ventilation. The site was a mound, which common sense, instead of levelling, would have utilized as a plinth. I pointed this out to the Executive Engineer, but he blandly assured me that what had been done was quite according to rule, and that it was only the Babu's perverseness which made him refuse to live there.

As a benevolent institution, the Hospital and Dispensary yields to none in the Province. In 1882 as many as 898 surgical operations were performed in it, including 363 for cataract; and in 1883 the total number rose still higher, to 1,010. These splendid results were due to the skill and devotion of Dr. Willcocks, the Civil Surgeon, who, by his intimate acquaintance with the language, kindliness of manner and inexhaustible patience, combined with remarkable success in treatment, had acquired a great reputation, which attracted patients from all the surrounding districts.

The school is a spacious vaulted room with broad verandahs and a curiously ugly campanile, which, as in the Tahsili School already mentioned, suggests the idea of a non-conformist chapel. It was originally intended to accommodate only a hundred boys, and as the number of pupils at the beginning of this year had risen to 176, an additional class-room became imperatively necessary, and this has now been supplied. It covers almost exactly the same area as the old building, but is in a very different style of architecture, with a high flat roof—to which access is gained by a picturesque stair-turret—a well raised plinth, cut-brick arcaded walls, stone traceried windows, and handsomely carved doors. The cost will be about Rs. 4,500, of which sum more than half comes from an endowment bestowed upon the school by Saiyid Mihrbán Ali, who is always foremost in the support of every deserving local institution. The Superintending Engineer's official criticism of the new room is highly characteristic. He condemns it as "quite out of keeping with the original building and defective in design." Architects and art critics in London and New York apparently find something to admire in the new works at Bulandshahr, and gladly go to considerable expense in procuring models and drawings of them; but the taste of our provincial Vitruvius is far more fastidious, and can only be satisfied by the elegant refinements of his own departmental standards.

In the same compound stands a boarding house, where such of the boys are lodged as have no relations with whom they can live in the town. There is now accommodation for forty. The building is in the form of a quadrangle, of which about one-half was finished and occupied before I took charge of the district. It was simply a barrack of the very plainest description, and for the sake of uniformity I was obliged to continue it on somewhat similar lines. But I have given it character by adding a gateway in the centre of one wing, throwing out two stair-turrets at the corners of the front, and substituting pierced stone-tracery for wooden bars in the windows. An extension at the back has also been made this year and over this at some future time, when sanction has been obtained, it would give importance to the design, if a large dormitory were added as an upper story. The existing accommodation is still inadequate, and a house has to be rented in the town for some of the boys. There is an available fund of Rs. 2,000 invested in Government paper, the interest of which is spent upon scholarships. But the craving for English education among the poorer classes already amounts almost to a disease, and, in my opinion, ought not to be encouraged by a system of gratuitous education. From the very beginning of my career I have been an enthusiast for a certain kind of schooling, but I am convinced that the study of English has been pushed on too rapidly. Being regarded simply as a means for making a livelihood, it is not the leaders of native society, but only the struggling and the indigent who are anxious to secure Government education for their sons. When they have completed the first stage of the appointed curriculum, they can seldom afford to proceed any further, and—in order to support themselves—begin to look out for employment. As the general civilization of the country is only in the agricultural stage, native society does not require their services: the only patron to whom they can turn is Government, and every Government office is already besieged by a host of disappointed candidates. The ideal condition of things would be an English-speaking and highly cultivated aristocracy, with a proletariat able to read and write their own vernacular, and a middle class further instructed either in English, if they aim at being clerks, or in technique, if they would become intelligent artisans. The actual results of the system of low fees and profuse scholarships are the reverse of the above, and the whole framework of society is in consequence disorganized. The poor learn absolutely too much; the rich, too little; while the middle classes waste their time over what is relatively useless, being incongruous with their special rôle in life.

The mention of stone-traceried windows may have been noticed in the above description of the new school buildings, and the introduction of such a feature may possibly strike some people as an unnecessary extravagance. But the use of glass in a school-room is, to my mind, an example of the unthinking prejudice against oriental fashions which characterizes the whole action of the Public Works Department. Nothing could be more unsuitable: with English boys running in and out, the window-doors of the regulation pattern would not have a whole pane left in one of them by the end of the first week after the holidays. Hindu lads are much quieter and more sedate, but—even so—breakages are frequent, and to obviate the cost of repairs the Superintending Engineer, in his inspection reports, always recommends that whenever glass is broken, it should be replaced with tin. A more clumsy expedient it would be difficult to conceive. The patch-work has a most beggarly appearance, and the tin of course is not transparent. The more sensible plan, and the one entirely in accord with eastern ideas, is that which I have adopted, in making the doors of solid carpentry and introducing light by means of windows set higher in the walls and fitted with ornamental tracery. In the Tahsili school, where the old windows were of large dimensions and reached to the ground, I have filled them in with wooden lattice-work as being cheaper than stone. They give free admission to the air and subdue without materially obstructing the light, while they are further provided with inside shutters, which can be closed in case of a storm. The initial cost is rather heavier, but it is eventually recovered by the saving on repairs. The artistic effect will probably be regarded as another objection by the typical engineer, who is possessed with the lamentable delusion, that nothing can be good unless it is also ugly, and who treats a school as a purely utilitarian building. It appears to me, on the contrary, that the cultivation of the taste is an important element in any system of mental training, and that it is a matter for unqualified regret that the natives of the country, from their earliest childhood, should be taught to associate the idea of all that is mean and shabby with the British Government. The effect lasts throughout life. Hence the educated natives' adoption of everything that is ugliest in European dress and equipment, and the necessity that he feels for an apology whenever he relapses into conformity with the prescriptions of oriental good taste. It is done—as he explains—out of regard for the prejudices of his women-folk, or of his less enlightened kinsmen.

The large and costly buildings, of which special mention has been made, by no means exhaust the list of improvements in the town. They are the most calculated to catch the eye of a complete stranger; but a former habitué, who returns after an interval of eight or nine years, is perhaps still more struck by the astonishing transformation of the ordinary shops and dwelling houses. As many as 870 of these have been pulled down and rebuilt. Formerly they were of mud with the floor a foot or more below the level of the street, and with thatched roofs always liable to catch fire. The debris of the old structure now forms a raised plinth, the walls are of brick, and beams support a flat roof which forms a healthy sleeping-place. Many of these tenements are occupied by the labouring classes, who have built them with their own hands, and of course their architectural pretensions are very slight. But a little simple ornamentation about the doorways or the eaves generally redeems them from absolute bareness, and renders them not unpleasing to the eye. In fact, many a Lodha and Chamár has now a more serviceable and a better looking house of his own construction, than is provided by Government for its subordinate officials.

As the Supreme Government has greatly at heart the check of epidemic disease among the urban population by the introduction of more adequate sanitary arrangements, it is not unusual for its periodical review of Municipal administration to conclude with a paragraph, urging Committees to devote a larger part of their annual income to drainage schemes. This is passed on through the regular official channel, and eventually reaches the District officer with a docket from his immediate superior, calling his special attention to the subject. As the Service prides itself on its loyalty, and a character for unquestioning submission to authority is considered one of the most approved claims to promotion, he at once allots a large sum for new drains in the next year's budget. The project is forthwith sanctioned as a commendable indication of public spirit, the drains are dug, and remain a nuisance ever afterwards. It is entirely forgotten that there is a vast difference between drains and drainage. In a dry climate, like that of Northern India, where it rains on an average only about twenty-five days in the year, there can be no constant excess of moisture to provide against. A covered drain is at all times and in every country the chosen home of typhoid, while a deep open drain is for 340 days, out of the whole 365, a dangerous pitfall or a slovenly dust-bin. Even when the rare and sudden flood does come, it has its own way very much as before, for any ordinary channel must be inadequate to contain it. The proper method is to have broad paved or metalled streets with an almost imperceptible slope from one end to the other, and also from the centre to the sides, so that the water may rapidly run off without the necessity for any drain whatever. Every improvement in the town of Bulandshahr during the last six years has had a beneficial effect on the drainage; but on actual drains nothing has been spent except in closing, or at least raising the level of those which had been constructed by my predecessors, and upon which the whole Municipal income would appear to have been squandered. Certainly, beyond drains and latrines, there were no other visible results of Municipal administration; for the dispensary and school had been built out of special funds, to which the Municipality did not even contribute.

All the new improvements have been designed and successfully carried out by independent local agency, never with the slightest assistance from departmental quarters, but for the most part in the face of much professional opposition. On the other hand, the performances of the trained engineers in Government service make a very insignificant appearance. The local works, which they have executed during the last fifty years, have been simply as follows:—The Jail; the District Law Courts; the Lowe Memorial; the Assistant Surgeon's official quarters; the Church and the Church Chaukidar's Lodge. The last named can only be regarded as a practical joke. The Church itself, which stands at the extreme west end of the station, was completed in 1864 at a cost of Rs. 5,750, on which the contractor, Mr. Michell, now a large landed proprietor in the Merath district, is said to have been a considerable loser. The money was raised by a subscription, which had been headed by Mr. Lowe, the then Collector, a son-in-law of the Lieutenant-Governor, Sir William Muir. He died in July 1862, and is buried in the Chancel. His name is further commemorated by a colonnaded building in the Cucherry compound, called the Lowe Memorial, which is used as a place of shelter for people attending the courts. They, no doubt, find it a convenience, and the design is for the most part too simple to criticise, except for the low square clock-tower, which is obtrusively ugly and ill-proportioned. The diminutive battlements, with which it is crowned, were doubtless intended to give it a Gothic character, but only emphasize its want of any architectural character whatever. The cost was Rs. 6,936. As usual, there was no access to the roof, except by a break-neck ladder, till 1878, when I added a corner stair-turret. The Church is rather a pretty little building, and as a far-away imitation of Gothic, is more successful on the whole than Indian churches frequently are. It is crushed by a low vaulted roof of very un-Gothic type, and in order to resist its thrust, the buttresses, which are very short, have such a wide straddle as to give the whole composition a touch of the grotesque. The Lodge, added in 1883, is a reproduction of the mother-building on the most diminutive scale, and is more like a doll's house than a structure intended for human habitation. It has a very high-pitched roof, with miniature buttresses and pointed arches to the doors and windows, and is divided into two rooms, corresponding to a nave and chancel, the internal dimensions of which are respectively nine and six feet square! As a fanciful addition to the Church grounds it may have its merits; but it is quite certain that the Chaukidar, for whose comfort it was built, will never consent to immure himself in such a cramped and stifling prison. As regards the other engineer-works: the Jail, first built in 1835, but enlarged in 1845 and again in 1883, is a straggling range of barracks, which the most ordinary village mason could have constructed; the Law Courts are not only of the meanest appearance, but are also altogether inadequate in accommodation: the rooms provided for the Sessions Judge may be specially mentioned as in the hot weather absolutely uninhabitable. The same is the case with the Assistant Surgeon's house. In the schools, dispensary and post-office, the workmanship, which is good, was non-professional; the designs were supplied by the department and are certainly, open to exception. Such are the facts, and the conclusion to which they point is surely this, that the district would have been a direct gainer, both as regards the possession of more sightly public buildings and in the greater encouragement of local industry and talent, if it had been allowed to provide for its own wants in its own way, without any inter-meddling at all on the part of the Government bureau.

In the three outlying Municipalities of Khurja, Anupshahr and Sikandarabad, it has not been found possible to insist upon an equal attention to minutiæ, or to secure the same air of congruity as pervades the streets and bazars of Bulandshahr. Though Khurja is by far the largest and richest town in the district, and several of its principal citizens have handsome dwelling-houses with gate ways and façades of carved stone, these indications of wealth are, for the most part, buried away in the back lanes and alleys, while the sides of the main thoroughfares continue to be disfigured with mud walls and unsightly excrescences, which the native members of the Committee are too apathetic to set themselves to abolish. In each of the three towns, however, some one large scheme has been successfully accomplished. Even at Anupshahr, which has an annual income of little more than Rs. 6,000, by dint of economy it has been found possible to provide funds for the construction of a large and handsome Saráe in the form of a quadrangle, with vaulted cells and corridors and a fine entrance gateway, over which will be built a Committee Room as at Bulandshahr. The cost has been Rs. 9,200, and it brings in an annual return of Rs. 250. At Sikandarabad, which lies in a hollow, and had suffered terribly from fever, a great improvement in the public health has been effected by an expenditure of Rs. 4,150 on an extensive system of drainage. The channel, which is in five branches, with a total length of 7½ miles, makes a complete circuit of the town and has its ultimate outfall in a natural water-course. The large sum of Rs. 12,500 has also been allotted for a Town Hall, still in course of erection. The doors, which are entirely the work of local carpenters, are of remarkably handsome design and careful execution. Being greatly admired by visitors, they have had an important effect in stimulating the revival of a decaying art, and now the traders in the principal bazar are vying with one another in the excellence of the carved arcades with which they are ornamenting their shop fronts, and which promise to render the street one of the most picturesque in the district. The movement is entirely spontaneous, and shows what an immense influence for good in the encouragement of indigenous arts and industries might be exercised by Municipal Committees if only they had more liberty of action than is often accorded them, and were not compelled to submit their designs for the sanction of a department which abominates individuality.

At Khurja the new market-place and bazar may fairly claim to be the finest modern architectural group of the kind in the Province. The market is in the form of a quadrangle, entirely fronted with carved stone, and has two entrance gates, of which the larger is 36 feet high, 40 feet broad, and as much as 60 feet deep, with a double story of arcades on either side under its lofty roof, as in the portals of the old Imperial Forts, at Agra and Delhi. In the centre of the square is a mosque, which on market days seriously obstructs the crowded area, and at all times is felt to be out of harmony with its environment, both because it stands at a different angle from the surrounding shops, and also because all the latter are occupied exclusively by Hindus. Before the site was cleared, a fakir had a mud hut here, which he represented to be a religious edifice and protested against its conversion to secular uses. The matter was taken up by an ignorant and factious crew of Pathâns, who muster strong in the town; and for fear of being thought lukewarm in the faith, the more respectable and better educated members of the Muhammadan community were o liged to side with the multitude. In order to prevent a disturbance, permission to rebuild the mosque had therefore to be accorded, but it was accompanied with the condition that it should be of stone and of handsome design. The largest amount of ornamentation has been bestowed upon its back wall, for this is directly opposite the main gate. It is an elaborate piece of panelling, and from the street, under the great arch, looks well as a screen at the end of the vista. On any other site—and many others were offered—the mosque would have been more useful for religious purposes, and architecturally would have reflected credit on the good taste of the Muhammadan community; standing where it does, it serves only as a memorial of their irrational and intolerant fanaticism. The shops on one side of the square are of great depth and have a double frontage, looking out at the back on to a new street nearly two furlongs in length, which, beginning with a width of 40 feet, sweeps round in a curved line till it again joins the main thoroughfare. The end of it last completed had previously been only from 6 to 8 feet wide. Even so, it was the most frequented bazar in the town, and the shops were a valuable property, for which heavy compensation had to be awarded. The entire cost of this extensive undertaking has been over Rs. 80,000, of which Rs. 14,000 were spent on the gates.

Khurja can also boast of a spacious tank with an aqueduct, a mile in length, by which it is filled from the Ganges Canal. It makes a fine sheet

MARKET SQUARE, KHURJA.
SIDE ENTRANCE.

of water, and at two of its corners has pretty stone kiosques, the gift of the resident Honorary Magistrate, Kunvar Azam Ali Khán. The two at the opposite angle are now being added at a further cost of Rs. 1,200 by the Municipality, which has also defrayed the total expenditure on the tank itself and the aqueduct which, together, amounted to Rs. 18,000.

Of all public improvements a tank is perhaps the one which the people of India most highly appreciate, and they are always ready to contribute to its construction to the full extent of their means. Besides the two at Khurja and Bulandshahr, eight* others have been made in smaller towns in the district, at an aggregate cost of Rs. 20,000; a nucleus in each case, large or small, being first collected by the people on the spot, and then supplemented by grants from local funds. The same system has been adopted with regard to new schools. If the people of any locality take sufficient interest in the matter to contribute half the cost, the District Board provides the other moiety, the school is built, and the villagers, having invested some of their own money in it, generally evince a more lasting zeal for its success than if it had been an entirely free gift. If a similar method were more widely practised throughout the country, local improvements and local public spirit would be developed on a far more solid basis, than by the institution of any number of elective committees.

The above long record of local improvements can scarcely be regarded as otherwise than a remarkable one for a single district to exhibit during the brief space of six years. Probably not one tithe of similar work has been executed in the same time in any corresponding part of the Province, where action has been strictly regulated by departmental routine. If so, the point for which I contend is practically established. The tyranny of departmentalism, and the servitude of the individual as now practised, are not only unnecessary in the interests either of the Government or the people, but are positively injurious to both. The remedy for present evils lies in local self-Government, which—rightly understood—is the greatest blessing that could be conferred on the country. Its requirements, however, are not satisfied by the mere introduction of an ingenious scheme for the election of representative members to form such a Board as that hitherto

---

* These eight towns are Aurangabad, Jewar, Dibhái, Járcha, Jhájhar, Kakor, Dankor, and Rabupura. At the last-named the work was a restoration of an old tank, which had fallen into ruin. The others were all entirely new.

existing, which, when once constituted, has no further functions to discharge but such as are purely ornamental, with no resources to develope, no funds of its own to administer, and no independence of action. Its nominal servants are its actual masters, who are appointed by an external department, are under its orders and look to it for promotion. The control over accounts is so vexatiously minute, and the returns which have to be supplied are so voluminous, that their despatch to the central bureau at Allahabad costs the Committee Rs. 300 a year simply for postage stamps, while the pay of the clerical establishment makes an annual charge of at least Rs. 5,000. Such a Board is simply a screen for the most exaggerated form of centralization. The system is wasteful, demoralizing and inefficient. On the other hand, fiscal and administrative economy would be secured, the character of the people would be elevated, and material progress advanced, if every district had the management of its own funds, acting under the guidance of its natural leaders, unhampered by departmental interference, forming its own projects and employing its own agency. Projects, before commencement, would require the general sanction of superior authority, and on completion would be submitted to the severest scrutiny. But the details of execution should be trusted to local intelligence, without undue insistence on technical refinements; and the work itself, as inspected on the spot, should be the test of success, not the figured statements as deposited in the Central bureau. Bulandshahr is in no way an exceptionally favourable district for internal development. A precisely parallel work has been simultaneously in progress at Murár, where—under the direction of General Dunham Massy—the Regimental Bazar, which was formerly as mean and squalid as such places generally are, has been converted into a handsome town with broad and well-built streets. For cleanliness, convenience and architectural propriety, it is now a perfect model of what the native quarter of an Indian Cantonment should be. Similarly, throughout India there are hands ready to work, and money waiting to be spent on improvements that every one desires, but which for the most part are never undertaken for want of a little active sympathy and co-operation on the part of the local authorities, who—for all their good will—are cowed into inaction by the incubus of an arbitrary and overbearing department.

NOTE.—Illustrations of some of the buildings mentioned in this Chapter appeared in No. ~~IV~~ of the *Journal of Indian Art*, edited by Mr. Kipling, the Principal of the Lahor School of Art.

APPENDIX.

A. LIST OF SUBSCRIBERS TO THE BATHING GHA'T.

No.	Name	Rs.	a.	p.
1	Saiyid Mír Khán, Sardár Bahádur, of Khánpur, ...	1,200	0	0
2	Nawáb Muhammad Mahmúd Ali Khán, Bahádur, of Chatári, ...	1,000	0	0
3	Kunvar Muhammad Abdullah Khán, of Dharmpur,...	1,000	0	0
4	Muhammad Ismáil Khán, of Malakpur, ...	800	0	0
5	Nawáb Sir Muhammad Faiz Ali Khán, Bahádur, K. C. S. I., of Pahásu, ...	500	0	0
6	Saiyid Bákir Ali Khán, C. I. E., of Pindráwal, ...	500	0	0
7	Ráo Umráo Singh, of Kuchesar, ...	500	0	0
8	Chaudhari Lachhman Singh, of Shikárpur, ...	500	0	0
9	Munshi Lachhman Sarúp, of Sikandarabad	500	0	0
10	Kunvar Khushál Singh, of Sáhanpur	500	0	0
11	Ráo Maháráj Singh, of Sarai Chhabílá	500	0	0
12	Kunvar Muhammad Abdul Rahmán Khán, of Dharmpur,	300	0	0
13	Kunvar Mashúk Ali Khán, of Dánpur, ...	250	0	0
14	Nawáb Muhammad Ali Khán, of Jahángirabád, ...	250	0	0
15	Kunvar A'zam Ali Khán, of Khurja, ...	250	0	0
16	Muhammad Imdád Ali Khán, of Khailiá, ...	200	0	0
17	Munshi Mihrbán Ali, of Guláuthi, ...	200	0	0
18	Munshi Khushi Rám, of Bhatona, ...	200	0	0
19	Saiyid Khán-shírin Khán, of Khánpur, ...	200	0	0
20	Lálá Sikla Mal, of Khurja, ...	200	0	0
21	Saiyid Muhammad Khán, of Daulatpur, ...	100	0	0
22	Maulvi Muhammad Bakhsh, of Chaprávat, ...	100	0	0
23	Pír-jí Muhabbat Ali, of Kádiri Bágh, ...	100	0	0
24	Muhammad Ahmad Ali Khán, of Khurja, ...	100	0	0
25	Muhammal Hurmat Khán, of Pindráwal, ...	100	0	0
26	Saiyids Shaffakat Ali and Muhabbat Ali, of Aurangabad,	100	0	0
27	Chaube Bhairon Prasád, of Bulandshahr, ...	100	0	0
28	Saiyid Jívan Ali, of Aurangabad, ...	100	0	0
29	Lálá Bansidhar, of Khurja, ...	100	0	0

		Rs.	a.	p.
30	Chaudhari Kishan Singh, of Sehra, ...	100	0	0
31	Lálá Johri Mal, of Bulandshahr, ...	100	0	0
32	Muhammad Abdul-Rahmán Khán, of Basai,... ..	50	0	0
33	Muhammad Abdullah Khán, of Kanársi, ...	50	0	0
34	Muhammad Umar Khán, of Khurja, ...	50	0	0
35	Muhammad Ahmad Khán, of Khurja,...	50	0	0
36	Muhammad Ahmad Khán II, of Khurja, ...	50	0	0
37	Muhammad Abdul-Rahmán Khán, of Khurja, ...	50	0	0
38	Thákur Harsaháe Singh, of Jewar, ...	50	0	0
39	Lálá Shádi Rám, of Sayána, ...	50	0	0
40	Seth Achal Dás, of Sikandarabad, ...	50	0	0
41	Kunvar Beni Krishan, of Sikandarabad, ...	50	0	0
42	Mirza Ibráhim Beg, of Khurja, ...	50	0	0
43	Haridwar Gir, Gosain, of Jahángirabád, ...	50	0	0
44	Muhammad Ghulám Kádir Khán, of Chanderu, ...	50	0	0
45	Residents in the town of Bulandshahr, ...	1,404	0	0
	Total Rs. ...	12,704	0	0

The balance was contributed by the Municipality.

B. LIST OF SUBSCRIBERS TO THE LYALL TANK.

No.	Name		Rs.	a.	p.
1	Saiyid Mír Khán, Sardár Bahádur, of Khánpur,	...	2,200	0	0
2	Kunvar Muhammad Abdul Ali Khán, of Chatári,	...	2,000	0	0
3	Kunvar Muhammad Faiyáz Ali Khán, of Pahásu	...	1,000	0	0
4	Kunvar Abdul Ghafúr Khán, of Dharmpur,	...	1,000	0	0
5	Saiyid Mihrbán Ali, of Guláuthi, ...	...	1,000	0	0
6	Chaube Bishambhar Náth, of Bulandshahr. ...	...	600	0	0
7	Nawáb Muhammad Ali Khán, of Jahángirabád,	...	500	0	0
8	Ráo Umráo Singh, of Kuchesar, ...	...	500	0	0
9	Chaudhari Lachhman Singh, of Shikárpur, ...	...	500	0	0
10	Munshi Lachhman Sarúp, of Sikandarabad, ...	...	500	0	0
11	Kunvar Máshúk Ali Khán, of Dánpur, ...	...	500	0	0
12	Muhammad Imdád Ali Khán, of Khailia, ...	...	500	0	0
13	Kunvar A'zam Ali Khán, of Khurja, ...	...	500	0	0
14	Ráni Mahtáb Kunvar, widow of the late Rao Maháráj Singh, of Sarái Chhabíla, ...	...	400	0	0
15	Muhammad Ghulám Haidar Khán, of Chanderu,	...	250	0	0
16	Lálas Imrat Lál and Amolak Chand, of Khurja,	...	250	0	0
17	Saiyid Muhammad Khán, of Daulatpur, ...	...	200	0	0
18	Muhammad Ahmad Ali Khán, of Khurja, ...	...	200	0	0
19	Chaudhari Kishan Singh, of Sehra, ...	...	200	0	0
20	Chaudhari Karan Singh, of Sikri, ...	...	200	0	0
21	Thákur Harsaháe Singh, of Jewar, ...	...	200	0	0
22	Lálá Joti Prasád, of Semli, ...	...	200	0	0
23	Saiyid Hurmat Khán, of Pindráwal, ...	...	150	0	0
24	Saiyid Jívan Ali, of Aurangabad, ...	...	150	0	0
25	Maulvi Muhammad Bakhsh, of Chaprávat, ...	...	100	0	0
26	Pír-jí Muhabbat Ali, of Kádiri Bágh, ...	...	100	0	0
27	Kunvar Tára Singh, of Jahángirabád, ...	...	100	0	0
28	Muhammad Abdul-Rahmán Khán, of Khurja,	...	100	0	0
29	Saiyids Muhabbat Ali and Shaffakat Ali, of Aurangabad,		100	0	0
30	Lálá Bansidhar, of Khurja, ...	...	100	0	0
31	Saiyid Ján, of Bulandshahr, ...	...	70	0	0
32	Muhammad Abdul-Rahmán Khán, of Basai,...	...	50	0	0
33	Muhammad Abdul-Karím Khán, of Kanársi,	...	50	0	0
34	Saiyid Zulfikár Ali, of Aurangabad, ...	...	50	0	0

35	Saiyid Muhammad Zaman, of Aurangabad, ...	50	0	0
36	Mirza Ibrahim Beg, of Khurja, ...	50	0	0
37	Lálá Jánaki Prasád, of Khurja, ...	50	0	0
38	Lálá Lekh Ráj, of Khurja, ...	50	0	0
39	Lálás Sant Lál and Moti Lál, of Khurja, ...	50	0	0
40	Lálá Lachhman Dás, of Khurja, ...	50	0	0
41	Lálá Bansidhar II., of Khurja, ...	25	0	0
42	Lálá Jwálá Datt, of Khurja, ...	25	0	0
43	Saiyid Kurbán Husain, of Aurangabad, ...	25	0	0
	Total Rs. ...	14,895	0	0

The balance was paid from Municipal funds.